The Pervasive Role of Science, Technology, and Health in Foreign Policy

Imperatives for the Department of State

D1086916

Committee on Science, Technology, and Health Aspects of the
Foreign Policy Agenda of the United States

Office of International Affairs
National Research Council

NATIONAL ACADEMY PRESS
Washington, D.C.

NATIONAL ACADEMY PRESS · 2101 Constitution Ave., N.W. · Washington, D.C. 20418

NOTICE: The project that is the subject of this report was approved by the Governing Board of the National Research Council, whose members are drawn from the councils of the National Academy of Sciences, the National Academy of Engineering, and the Institute of Medicine. The members of the committee responsible for the report were chosen for their special competencies and with regard for appropriate balance.

This project was sponsored by the Golden Family Foundation and the Carnegie Corporation of New York. Any opinions, findings, conclusions, or recommendations expressed in this publication are those of the authors and do not necessarily reflect the view of the organizations or agencies that provided support for the project. The Golden Family Foundation and the Carnegie Corporation do not take responsibility for any statements or views expressed.

International Standard Book Number 0-309-06785-5

A limited number of copies of this report are available from:

Office for Central Europe and Eurasia
National Research Council
2101 Constitution Avenue, N.W. FO2060
Washington, D.C. 20418
Tel: (202) 334-2644

Copies of this report are available for sale from:

National Academy Press
2101 Constitution Avenue, N.W. Box 285
Washington, D.C. 20055
Tel: 1-800-624-6242 or (202) 334-3313 (in the Washington Metropolitan Area).

COMMITTEE ON SCIENCE, TECHNOLOGY, AND HEALTH ASPECTS OF THE FOREIGN POLICY AGENDA OF THE UNITED STATES

Robert A. Frosch, *Chair*, Harvard University
John D. Axtell, Purdue University
Harry Barnes, The Carter Center
Gail H. Cassell, Eli Lilly & Co.
Sue E. Eckert, Institute for International Economics and Brown University
Robert W. Fri, The Smithsonian Institution
David Hamburg, Carnegie Corporation of New York
Ronald F. Lehman II, Lawrence Livermore National Laboratory
Thomas E. Lovejoy, The World Bank
David D. Newsom, University of Virginia
Roland W. Schmitt, Rensselaer Polytechnic Institute
Eugene B. Skolnikoff, Massachusetts Institute of Technology
Philip M. Smith, McGeary & Smith
Robert M. White, The Washington Advisory Group

Ex-officio Members

David Challoner, Foreign Secretary, Institute of Medicine
Harold Forsen, Foreign Secretary, National Academy of Engineering
F. Sherwood Rowland, Foreign Secretary, National Academy of Sciences

Staff

John Boright, Executive Director, Office of International Affairs
Glenn Schweitzer, Study Director
Kelly Robbins, Program Officer
Mickelle Rodgers, Program Assistant

Contents

Preface

ORIGIN AND BACKGROUND OF THE STUDY

In April 1998, the Department of State requested that the chairman of the National Research Council (NRC) initiate a study of the contributions that science, technology, and health (STH) expertise and activities can make in the formulation and implementation of foreign policy and of how the Department might better carry out its responsibilities to that end (see Appendix A). This request followed many months of informal discussions between the two organizations about the increasing importance of the STH aspects of foreign policy and the rapid growth of the related international interests of many U.S. government departments and agencies, industry, universities, and other nongovernmental organizations. Before undertaking a study, the NRC staff consulted with more than 20 senior officials of the Department who, without exception, indicated that they would be interested in considering the conclusions and recommendations to be developed. The Golden Family Foundation and the Carnegie Corporation of New York generously agreed to provide financial support for the study.

There had been growing criticism by U.S. scientists and foreign policy experts during congressional hearings and in *Science* and other publications of the inadequate attention being given to STH by the Department. In addition, in 1998 and 1999 the American Association for the Advancement of Science offered its suggestions for strengthening STH capabilities within the Department.[1] To many, it appeared that the Department was reducing its STH capabilities even though the STH dimensions of foreign policy were rapidly expanding. Concerns centered on the following actions by the Department:

- *Redirection of personnel resources that had been devoted to a broad range of STH activities to a more narrow emphasis on environmental diplomacy:* While environmental issues were growing in importance and additional resources were urgently needed to address emerging global environmental issues, other aspects of STH were also having an increased impact on foreign policy.
- *Elimination of the science and technology "cone" as one of the cones that provided the framework for assignments and promotion within the Foreign Service personnel system:* While the science and technology cone may have become a glass ceiling for some Foreign Service Officers (FSOs) with interests in STH-related issues, a more satisfactory approach to career development was not offered for these personnel.
- *Reduction in the number of Science Counselor[2] positions at U.S. embassies and filling of the remaining positions primarily with FSOs with little background in STH activities.*
- *Delay in providing leadership for the Bureau for Oceans and International Environmental and Scientific Affairs (OES), including a delay of more than 18 months in appointing the Assistant Secretary.*

Whatever the reasons for these actions or lack of actions, they were widely interpreted within the U.S. STH communities as signaling a decline of

---

[1]Information regarding relevant hearings held by the House Committee on Science in March 1998 may be found at http://www.house.gov/science/science_policy_study.htm. In addition, the Council of the American Association for the Advancement of Science (AAAS) passed a resolution entitled "Science and Technology Counselors at U.S. Embassies" in February 1998. Other AAAS officials have written to the Department on the issue, including AAAS Board of Directors Chair Mildred Dresselhaus, who wrote to the Secretary of State on October 23, 1998 (copy available from NRC Public Access Records Office, 202-334-3543). See also Anne Keatley Solomon, "The Science and Technology-Bereft Department of State," *Science* vol. 282 (November 1998): 1649-1650; J. Thomas Ratchford, "Put Science and Technology Back into Foreign Policy," *Science* vol. 282 (November 1998): 1650; James D. Watkins, "Science and Technology in Foreign Affairs," *Science* vol. 277 (August 1997): 650-651.

[2]Over the years the terminology used for specialists assigned by the Department to the embassies has varied—Science and Technology Counselors; Environmental, Science, and Technology Counselors; Science Attachés; Science Officers; and Environmental Officers, for example. For this report the titles of Science Counselors and Science Officers are used to include positions with slightly different names as well.

interest within the Department in activities that should be central aspects of the nation's foreign policy agenda.

As indicated in Appendix B, during the past four decades many studies have been undertaken on science, technology, and foreign policy. Studies sponsored by Congress have resulted in legislative mandates for enhancing the role of STH in the Department by establishing OES and by requiring annual reports to Congress on science, technology, and diplomacy. Although OES continues its activities, the annual reporting terminated in 1995. Other studies have been sponsored by the Department itself, particularly with regard to broadening activities within OES and to staffing U.S. embassies to address STH-related activities. During the past 15 years, the National Academies also have carried out a number of studies of selected aspects of STH and foreign policy. Other nongovernmental organizations and scholars have conducted relevant assessments. Of particular interest is a set of four reports directly related to the topic prepared in 1992 and 1993 by the Carnegie Commission on Science, Technology, and Government.

During the fall of 1998, the Henry L. Stimson Center released a report, *Equipped for the Future, Managing U.S. Foreign Affairs in the 21st Century*, and the Center for Strategic and International Studies issued a report, *Reinventing Diplomacy in the Information Age*. These reports address many aspects of the formulation and implementation of foreign policy; and they include some suggestions that are relevant to the STH dimension of foreign policy, particularly with regard to more effective use of information technologies within the Department and greater involvement of nongovernmental organizations and other private-sector institutions in the foreign policy process. In addition, for the past three years the U.S. Institute of Peace, in its Virtual Diplomacy Program, has promoted better understanding of the role of new information technologies in diplomacy.

A number of conclusions and recommendations included in this report were also set forth in earlier studies. Some were accepted and implemented by the Department for a period of time (e.g., technically trained Science Counselors at key embassies, an advisory committee on science and technology), but then the Department changed its approach. Others have been rejected altogether (e.g., organizational restructuring of the Department). Thus, the report may at times seem repetitious of previous efforts. The committee believes, however, that even if suggestions similar to its own recommendations have been rejected in the past, they should be raised again because of the rapid technological changes underway throughout the world, which call for new directions in the formulation and implementation of foreign policy. A key concern of the committee is to ensure that the changes recommended in this study, if accepted, are not simply temporary fixes but rather are institutionalized for the long term.

ROLE OF THE NRC COMMITTEE FOR THIS STUDY

In June 1998, the chairman of the NRC appointed a 17-member interdisciplinary committee to carry out this study. Biographies of committee members are included in Appendix C.

At the request of the Department, the committee issued a preliminary letter report in September 1998 so that recommendations could be considered in connection with the preparation of the Department's fiscal year 2000 budget request. The recommendations were directed to immediate and practical steps that the Department could take in two areas: *(1) providing leadership within the Department on STH-related issues* and (2) *strengthening the available base of STH expertise.*[3]

Following issuance of the preliminary report, the committee divided into three subcommittees to address the following topics in more detail: personnel policies and practices of the Department, with special attention to the STH aspects of these policies; the STH capabilities of selected bureaus and offices within the Department; and the effectiveness of the interactions between the Department and other government departments and agencies involved in international STH policies and programs (referred to as "other departments and agencies"). This report contains the findings and recommendations of the committee based largely on the work of the subcommittees as well as on other information available as of August 1999.

The committee has given special attention to the April 1999 announcement by Undersecretary for Global Affairs Frank Loy of five steps underway to strengthen the capabilities of the Department to address STH-related issues. These steps are

1. Appointment of a Science Advisor to the Secretary of State;

2. Organization of informal roundtable discussions of specific STH-related foreign policy issues involving both Department officials and distinguished members of the STH community;

3. Establishment at the Foreign Service Institute (FSI) of a short course in science and technology for new FSOs and a training program in environment, science, and technology for foreign nationals serving at U.S. embassies;

4. Long-term and short-term assignments within the Department of more scientists from the other departments and agencies and from academia; and

---

[3]See http://www.nap.edu/readingroom/books/sth for the entire report. The recommendations are set forth in Appendix D of this report.

5. Assessment of the relevance to current policies of each of the 33 bilateral science and technology "umbrella" agreements and evaluation of measures to improve the effectiveness of the environmental "hubs" where diplomats with responsibilities for reporting on environmental developments are stationed in various regions of the world.

These steps, if fully implemented, would be important in strengthening the Department's capabilities to deal effectively with STH-related issues while responding to several recommendations in the committee's preliminary letter report. However, there have been only limited activities within the Department to transform the announcement into action or to respond to other initial recommendations of the committee despite continuing discussions between the committee and the Department during the past year. The committee considers its initial recommendations to be still valid and important and therefore has incorporated them into this report as appropriate.

In June 1999, the Senate passed an amendment to the Department's authorization bill establishing the position of Science Advisor to the Secretary of State reporting through the Undersecretary for Global Affairs, with the Science Advisor's responsibilities to be determined by the Secretary. The amendment also requires the Department to provide a report to Congress on its plans for implementing the recommendations in this NRC report within six months of the report's release. In addition, the Senate bill includes a provision establishing the position of Assistant Secretary for Verification and Compliance reporting to the Undersecretary for Arms Control and International Security Affairs. This new position would provide an important interface between policy and STH concerns in one specific area. As of August 1999, this bill was awaiting action by the full Congress and the President (see Appendix E).

SCOPE OF THE REPORT

The committee considered the STH dimension of foreign policy in a broad sense and decided to concentrate its detailed investigations and recommendations on leadership within the Department in addressing issues with STH content, personnel policies and practices of the Department as they affect STH competence, STH capabilities of relevant bureaus and offices of the Department, and interactions of the Department with other departments and agencies involved in STH activities. The committee recognized that a very broad set of highly differentiated skills is needed to address the wide range of STH-related issues. The report indicates circumstances in which generalists are in a position to address such issues and sets forth a number of specific issues requiring more specialized expertise.

Throughout the process of preparing this report, the committee was mindful of the resource constraints faced by the Department. Indeed, Department officials repeatedly cited many competing priorities for additional resources, such as security requirements in U.S. embassies following the terrorist bombings of the embassies in Kenya and Tanzania, unanticipated humanitarian efforts in the wake of Hurricane Mitch, and resettlement activities in Kosovo. The committee appreciated current congressional reluctance to restore significant reductions in the government's international affairs budget that have been made in recent years. However, the case for strengthening the Department's STH capabilities is sufficiently compelling that modest immediate shifts of resources within the Department to begin to implement the committee's recommendations are fully warranted. For the longer term, the Department, in cooperation with the U.S. STH communities, should be able to provide Congress on a continuing basis with more persuasive evidence of the contribution of international STH activities to the security, political, and economic interests of the country and of the dangers from loss of U.S. leadership in many areas that can result from continuing to skimp on the STH-related resources available to the Department.

Also, the committee was aware of the major organizational and personnel adjustments taking place within the Department as the result of the incorporation of the Arms Control and Disarmament Agency (ACDA) and the U.S. Information Agency (USIA) into the Department and the likely reluctance within the Department and Congress to consider other far-reaching structural changes in the immediate future. Nevertheless, the committee considered that the interrelationships between STH developments and foreign policy are so profound that significant organizational and personnel adjustments will be essential in the years ahead, and this report offers recommendations concerning such changes. Initial steps along the lines recommended by the committee can be undertaken within the current organizational structure and personnel constraints. Meanwhile, planning for more extensive changes to meet the Department's expanded STH requirements should be undertaken promptly.

ACKNOWLEDGMENTS

Throughout the study, many government officials and nongovernmental specialists took time to help committee members and staff obtain important insights concerning a wide variety of opportunities and problems in the foreign policy process. A large number of offices of the Department were enormously helpful in providing information and suggestions concerning issues of interest to the committee. Similarly, a variety of other departments and agencies contributed valuable perspectives that were important in reaching the conclusions set forth in this report (see Appendix F).

This report has been reviewed in draft form by individuals chosen for their diverse perspectives and technical expertise, in accordance with procedures approved by the NRC's Report Review Committee. The purpose of such an independent review is to provide candid and critical comments that will assist the institution in making the published report as sound as possible and to ensure that the report meets institutional standards for objectivity, evidence, and responsiveness to the study charge. The review comments and draft manuscript remain confidential to protect the integrity of the deliberative process. We wish to thank the following individuals for their participation in the review of this report: John F. Ahearne, Sigma Xi Center; Frederick Bernthal, Universities Research Association, Inc.; Justin Bloom, Technology International; Lewis M. Branscomb, Harvard University; D. Allan Bromley, Yale University; Edward E. David, Jr., EED, Inc.; Gerald P. Dinneen, Honeywell Inc. (retired); E. A. Hammel, University of California, Berkeley; Rodney Nichols, New York Academy of Sciences; Princeton Lyman, Overseas Development Council; and Peter H. Raven, Missouri Botanical Garden. These individuals have provided constructive comments and suggestions, but it must be emphasized that responsibility for the final content of this report rests entirely with the authoring committee and the institution.

The committee expresses its appreciation to the many individuals and institutions that assisted in this effort. It also is grateful for the assistance of the NRC staff. Any errors in this report are the committee's own.

Robert A. Frosch, Chair, Committee on the Science, Technology, and Health Aspects of the Foreign Policy Agenda of the United States

Executive Summary

Issues involving science, technology, and health (STH) have moved to the forefront of the international diplomatic agenda. Other vital issues linked to technological developments pervade longer-range foreign policy concerns. Thus, STH considerations are often central to the Department of State's bilateral and multilateral interactions with other governments. STH aspects play a large role in discussions of such critical topics as nuclear nonproliferation, use of outer space, population growth, adequate and safe food supply, climate change, infectious diseases, energy resources, and competitiveness of industrial technologies. (See Box ES-1 for an expanded list of country- and region-specific issues with significant STH dimensions.) In addressing these issues, expert STH knowledge is essential to the anticipation and resolution of problems and to the achievement of foreign policy goals. The Department, recognizing that it requires strengthened capabilities to address such an array of topics, has asked for suggestions by the National Research Council as to how it could better deal with foreign policy issues with STH content.

America's unparalleled capabilities in STH are among the nation's strongest assets. The United States is at the leading edge of scientific discovery, has become a magnet for foreign graduate students in STH disciplines, and is the pacesetter for the world in high-technology exports. Also, American specialists are a cornerstone of the international STH communities, communities that share a common culture and common concerns across national borders and are thus themselves a force in international relations. These STH strengths of the nation can provide unparalleled support for the Department in the formulation and imple-

---

BOX ES-1
Examples of Issues with Significant STH Content and
Foreign Policy Relevance in Selected Countries and Regions

Russia
- Exports of missile and nuclear technologies
- Brain drain of former weaponeers and computer scientists
- Emergence of small innovative private firms
- Infectious diseases: AIDS, hepatitis, tuberculosis
- Participation in International Space Station
- Protection of nuclear materials and safety of nuclear reactors
- Y2K computer retrofits: military, aviation, and financial systems

China
- Energy mix and energy systems: coal, nuclear, hydropower; small stand-alone electrical grids
- Exports of military and dual-use technologies
- Population growth
- Development of space program
- Brain drain of students studying in United States
- Respect for intellectual property rights
- Adequate and safe food supply

Nigeria
- Oil exploration and exploitation
- Detection of drug trafficking
- Diseases: AIDS, river blindness, malaria
- Water and sewage treatment
- Population growth
- Nutrition deficiencies
- Brain drain of well-educated specialists

Mexico
- Breeding of wheat and corn varieties
- Sharing with United States of water resources
- Cultivation and trafficking of cocaine, marijuana, and synthetic drugs
- Compliance with pollution reduction requirements of the North American Free Trade Agreement
- Food safety and contamination of food exports

---

mentation of a foreign policy that will contribute to the creation of a more secure, prosperous, and democratic world for the benefit of the American people.

Precisely because STH developments are such a pervasive force, they cannot be isolated from the fundamental workings of foreign policy. The Department needs the capability to understand how technological factors

- Sewage discharges along Pacific coast
- Labor standards in high-tech industries

India
- Computer software capabilities
- Potential for nuclear weapons testing
- Population growth
- Biotechnology for agriculture and pharmaceuticals
- Adequate and safe food supply
- Trade with Russia in dual-use technologies
- $10 million program of U.S.-Indian S&T cooperation

Japan
- Foreign access to research facilities
- Emergence of high-tech terrorist groups such as Aum Shinrikyo
- Earthquake engineering
- Development of dual-use aerospace technologies
- Expansion of nuclear power industry, including use of plutonium
- Fishing activities: southern, northeastern, and northwestern Pacific Ocean
- Industrial competitiveness

European Union (regional)
- Genetically modified agricultural products
- Regulation of toxic chemicals
- Foreign access to research funds
- Export controls on computers
- Harmonization of laws on intellectual property rights
- Reconstruction of infrastructure in Balkans
- STH cooperation with nations of former USSR

Middle East (Jordan, Syria, Lebanon, Israel, Egypt, West Bank, and Gaza)
- Use of water resources: efficiency, desalination, recycling
- Biodiversity: flora and fauna
- Malnutrition: micronutrients, ciliac disease
- Communicable diseases: hepatitis
- Terrorism: transportation security, forensic investigations
- Population growth
- Waste disposal: water and sewage treatment and burial of hazardous wastes

influence political and economic developments. Indeed, an appreciation of how such factors are inextricably embedded in international relations is essential if the Department is to effectively avail itself of the expertise of the U.S. STH communities. More importantly, the Department must be equipped to reach its own conclusions, particularly when conflicting technical views are expressed by vested interests outside the Department.

Effective foreign policy must reflect a comprehensive approach within the Department to integrating STH competence into policy and program formulation and execution that rests on more concerted efforts in several areas:

- Increasing the sensitivity of all Foreign Service Officers (FSOs) and other Department officials to the relevance of STH considerations to foreign policy;
- Providing focused STH support at the highest levels of the Department, within several bureaus and offices, and at a number of embassies and missions to address current issues and to signal newly emerging issues;
- Establishing mechanisms that facilitate ready access by Department officials to the U.S. STH communities for advice on complex issues and for support during intergovernmental negotiations, major international conferences, and implementation of international programs; and
- Drawing on other departments and agencies to carry out STH activities that they are best equipped to address, thus enabling the Department to focus on the STH content that matters most for foreign policy.

Central to strengthening the capabilities of the Department in areas involving STH considerations is the need for a change in the orientation of the U.S. Foreign Service and indeed of the entire U.S. foreign policy community, which currently gives relatively little attention to STH considerations. To this end, the following interrelated recommendations are intended to stimulate an evolution of STH awareness within the Department. They emphasize the necessity for (1) leadership by the Secretary of State, (2) a strengthened organizational structure of the Department operating under the guidance of an Undersecretary of State, and (3) a motivated and informed workforce that will effectively address the multitude of STH-content issues during the next decade and beyond.

An essential first step in strengthening STH capabilities within the Department is a clear signal that the Secretary recognizes the significance of such capabilities, the importance of integrating informed STH considerations into foreign policy deliberations, and the need to strengthen STH capabilities. Also, the Secretary must demonstrate a commitment to taking steps to improve the Department's performance in carrying out its responsibilities that involve STH considerations. Thus, the first recommendation is critical and serves as the basis for the committee's further recommendations.

The Secretary should articulate and implement a policy that calls for greater attention to the STH dimensions of foreign policy throughout

the Department and provides guidance as to sources of STH expertise available to Department officials both in Washington and abroad. The Secretary's personal involvement is central to effecting substantial and lasting change within the Department. To this end, the Secretary should ensure that such a policy statement is regularly updated, widely disseminated, and coupled with an action agenda reflecting the recommendations set forth below. Implementation of these recommendations should proceed simultaneously on parallel but related tracks. (See page 25.)

The Department's leadership should expect all FSOs and other officials of the Department to achieve a minimum level of STH literacy and awareness relevant to foreign policy while stimulating attention to STH throughout the Department by establishing promotion and career incentives for successful service in STH-related positions.[1] In this regard, the Department should give greater attention to STH skills during the entrance examination for FSOs and expand the STH training offerings at the Foreign Service Institute (FSI) and elsewhere for both FSOs and civil servants. (See page 36.)

The Secretary should provide continuing leadership that ensures consideration within the Department of the STH aspects of issues. To this end, the Secretary should delegate to an undersecretary responsibility for ensuring consideration of STH factors in policy formulation, especially during meetings and consultations involving the Secretary and/ or the Secretary's senior advisors and during day-to-day activities at all levels of the Department. The title of the selected undersecretary should be amended to include the phrase "for Scientific Affairs," reflecting the new authority and responsibilities across a broad spectrum of STH aspects of foreign policy. The Secretary should make it clear that the oversight responsibilities of the undersecretary extend across the entire Department and involve coordinating the various clusters of STH expertise in the Department to provide an integrated approach to STH matters. The Undersecretary for Global Affairs currently has such responsibilities and should have the title of Undersecretary for Scientific and Global Affairs. Future secretaries, however, might consider that another undersecretary is the most appropriate official for assuming oversight responsibilities for STH activities. (See page 27.)

---

[1]STH literacy as used in this report includes an appreciation of basic STH concepts of importance for international affairs, knowledge of the responsibilities and capabilities of the key institutions that comprise the STH infrastructure of the United States, and familiarity with the principal international organizations and agreements that encompass STH developments at home and abroad.

The Secretary should select a highly qualified STH Senior Advisor to the Secretary and to the selected undersecretary to provide expert advice, drawing on the resources of the American STH communities, as necessary, on current and emerging issues. The STH Senior Advisor, with a rank and title appropriate to his or her responsibilities and an adequate staff, should be housed in the office of the undersecretary and should work with senior officials throughout the Department in identifying and addressing important policy and personnel issues and in mobilizing external support for STH activities, which could include consultations with Congress. The STH Senior Advisor should also serve as Executive Director of the STH Advisory Committee discussed below. (See page 28.)

The Department should adopt the most appropriate organizational structure for the relevant bureaus and offices in order to meet its expanding STH responsibilities. If legislation is necessary to accomplish this, the Department should seek congressional authorization. The current structure is inadequate for the task. The roles, responsibilities, and capabilities of the various undersecretaries and assistant secretaries to meet the broad range of STH challenges highlighted in this report should be the focal point of a Departmental review as the first step in implementing this recommendation. (See page 29.)

The Department should establish an STH Advisory Committee to the Secretary and take other steps to further expand the roster of external experts actively engaged in advising the Department's leadership on emerging STH-related issues. This advisory committee should take into account activities of other more specialized committees that exist in the national security and economics areas. Other external advisory mechanisms that also should be considered include (1) preparation of an expanded list of consultants who are kept current on STH issues of interest to the Department and who are called upon frequently, and (2) tasking of U.S. organizations outside government to mobilize expertise on selected topics as needed. (See page 29.)

The Department should increase the resources available to meet the essential STH-related requirements that are recommended in this report. The committee's interim report of September 1998 called for allocation of about a dozen new positions to expand STH-related activities in OES, the Policy Planning Staff (S/P), and the Bureau of Intelligence and Research (INR), and $500,000 annually to begin to support external advisory activities. In addition, adequate resources to support the STH Senior Advisor and a well-qualified staff are essential. Should major structural changes within the Department be required to meet future STH responsibilities, further resources will be needed. (See page 30.)

The Department should assign at least 25 carefully selected Science Counselors to embassies in countries where STH-related activities are of major interest to the U.S. Government and to missions to international and regional organizations that support STH programs of considerable foreign policy significance. The number of Science Counselor positions in embassies and missions has been reduced from 22 in the mid-1980s to 10, and whereas almost all of the 22 had strong technical backgrounds, few of the 10 current incumbents have such backgrounds. In order to reverse the recent decline in effective STH representation and reporting by key embassies, these Science Counselors should have strong educational backgrounds and experience in STH and should be sensitive to the needs of the departments and agencies in formulating foreign policy and in implementing international STH programs. These positions could be filled by specialists recruited from the civil service, universities, or industry, usually serving on a limited-term appointment basis, or by uniquely qualified FSOs. Many other embassies and missions also should be staffed with diplomats responsible for STH activities, but in most cases the positions can be filled by FSOs who have undergone significant training and orientation concerning U.S. STH interests and capabilities. (See page 57.)

The Department should increase its use of specialists from other departments and agencies as rotating employees assigned to positions in Washington and abroad, as participants in international negotiations, and as advisors on topics in their areas of expertise. The Department's leadership should have a continuing dialogue with senior officials of other departments and agencies on the mutual benefits from such involvement of technical personnel in its activities and should establish more effective mechanisms that will help ensure continued interagency support for addressing both ad hoc and recurring issues. (See page 72.)

The Department, in consultation with other departments and agencies, should transfer responsibilities for STH activities to other appropriate and willing departments and agencies whenever there is not a compelling reason for retaining responsibilities within the Department. The Department is overloaded in attempting to handle both the administrative and the substantive aspects of an ever-growing portfolio of international programs. By dispersing responsibilities to agencies capable of adequately handling them, the Department should be able to move toward a better balance of responsibilities and available resources. (See page 68.)

The Department, in consultation with the Office of Management and Budget (OMB) and other departments and agencies, should streamline the Circular 175 process, which calls for interagency reviews of proposed international agreements and bilateral memoranda of understanding (MOUs). The Department should address the criteria for determining the need for Circular 175 clearance, the appropriateness of sunset provisions for old and new MOUs, and procedures that will expedite preparation within the U.S. Government of satisfactory texts of proposed agreements and MOUs. Hundreds of STH agreements and MOUs are subject to Circular 175, and delays and inefficiencies in the process are a constant source of irritation among departments and agencies and sometimes create difficulties with foreign collaborators. (See page 69.)

The Secretary, the Administration, and Congress should ensure that the Department's five-year information technology modernization plan stays on course and is fully funded for its successful implementation and also for necessary ongoing maintenance and upgrades. Prompt implementation of the plan will not only reduce many internal communications problems repeatedly cited by Department officials but will provide greatly improved access to the information resources of the STH community. Also, the modernization program should improve the job satisfaction and productivity of many young employees who have grown up in the information age. (See page 46.)

These recommendations emphasize the importance of incorporating STH knowledge into the process of formulating and implementing foreign policy (*science for diplomacy*). At the same time, the Department has a responsibility to help facilitate the international programs and activities of Americans in both the public and the private sectors (*diplomacy for science*). As the Department strengthens its relationships with other organizations in formulating foreign policy, there will be many opportunities for close cooperation in furthering broad national interests through both science for diplomacy and diplomacy for science.

In sum, a comprehensive approach that expands opportunities within the Department for incorporating STH expertise into the foreign policy process and that provides stronger support for the international STH programs of a variety of departments and agencies and private-sector organizations can promote U.S. interests on many fronts. Given the U.S. strengths in STH, the Department can draw on unparalleled knowledge and on the hundreds of thousands of professional relationships that connect American specialists to the STH communities of other nations. To this end, the foregoing recommendations, together with additional recommendations set forth in subsequent chapters of this report, provide a basis for institutionalizing the effective use of the nation's STH capabilities as a fundamental element of foreign policy.

1

Integration of STH Developments and U.S. Foreign Policy

STH AT THE FOREFRONT OF DIPLOMACY

Issues involving science, technology, and health (STH) have moved to the forefront of the international diplomatic agenda. Other vital issues linked to technological developments pervade longer-range foreign policy concerns. Thus, the Department must interact with other governments at a large number of bilateral and multilateral forums where STH considerations are central to the deliberations. STH aspects play a large role in discussions of such critical topics as nuclear nonproliferation, the use of outer space, population growth, adequate and safe food supply, infectious diseases, energy resources, and competitiveness of industrial technologies. In short, expert STH knowledge is essential in assessing many bilateral issues, global developments, and interactions between countries of importance to the United States. Further indicating the pervasiveness of STH developments, 13 of the 16 objectives set forth in the U.S. *Strategic Plan for International Affairs* encompass STH considerations (see Appendix G). At the operational level, Box 1-1 presents a few examples of specific issues in which achievement of foreign policy goals has required an understanding of the STH elements of the issues.

Not surprisingly, STH developments are frequently entwined in decisions on broad issues confronting the Secretary of State and other senior officials of the Department; and they have become daily fare for many action officers throughout the Department and overseas. There are few U.S. embassies or substantive bureaus or offices in Washington that are not regularly involved in STH-related issues.

BOX 1-1
Recent Foreign Policy Issues with Significant STH Content

Communications Satellites and Technology Transfer

In the fall of 1998, the U.S. Senate reviewed the decisions of the Department of Commerce to provide licenses to U.S. manufacturers for launching U.S.-made communications satellites and foreign satellites with U.S.-made components on Chinese rockets. The point of contention was whether the space launch activities had significantly benefited China's missile or military satellite capabilities.

In looking to the future, the discussion centered on whether the Department of Commerce, with its major interest in promoting U.S. commercial sales, was the appropriate department to issue licenses for a technology with such obvious military relevance, whatever the safeguards to protect the technology. Late in 1998, Congress decided to transfer the licensing authority back to the Department of State.

Given the growing importance of space-based communications systems throughout the world and the commercial stakes involved, this type of controversy over sales versus national security will continue for the indefinite future.

U.S. Sanctions on Russian Scientific Institutions

During 1998-1999, the U.S. Government, acting on recommendations of the Department of State, determined that a number of Russian institutions were transferring technology of relevance to weapons of mass destruction and advanced conventional weapons to Middle Eastern countries. In view of the seriousness of such transfers, the government imposed prohibitions on U.S. procurement of goods, technologies, or services from these institutions; U.S. assistance to the institutions; and imports of goods, technology, or services from these institutions into the United States. The first determination was that seven of the institutions had transferred or planned to transfer missile-related items to Iran, the second was that three had transferred or planned to transfer nuclear-related or missile-related items to Iran, and the third was that three had transferred or planned to transfer lethal armaments to Syria.

Each of these determinations involved a decision that the technology transfer reached a level of concern that warranted stopping ongoing cooperative programs designed to advance U.S. national security through engagement of Russian institutions in programs of mutual interest. The technical judgments as to the gains to the potential recipients of the transfers required sophisticated understanding of the problems involved in designing and manufacturing advanced weapons systems. Further, judgments as to the scientific and technological losses to the United States from proposed termination of cooperation were important.

Removal of Uranium from Kazakhstan

In 1994, the American Ambassador in Almaty received a request from the Kazakh Government to provide assistance in disposing of weapons-grade highly enriched uranium left over from the Soviet era. The Ambassador, in close consultation with the Department and other U.S. Government departments and agencies, helped orchestrate a complicated, highly classified response that led to the transfer of 600 kilograms of uranium to Oak Ridge, Tennessee, thereby removing a potential proliferation problem. The operation, called Project Sapphire, was carried out with a minimum of problems in dealing with Russia, the U.S. Congress, and environmental groups.

The Ambassador had considerable previous experience in addressing nuclear issues—within the Department, in Geneva, and in Brazil. His background was one of the reasons for his assignment to Almaty, which proved to be a very astute move by the Department.

Global Climate Change

There is an international scientific consensus that greenhouse gases impede the outward flow of infrared radiation from the earth to such an extent that the result is a warming of the earth, its atmosphere, and its oceans. However, there is great controversy over the extent, timing, and significance of this warming and the costs and effectiveness of measures that might be undertaken to reduce the warming.

The Department is in continuing consultation with a number of congressional committees, several dozen U.S. departments and agencies, and many industrial, academic, and nongovernmental organizations as to steps that should be taken internationally to address global warming. Because of the scientific uncertainty and the potentially high costs of steps that might reduce adverse impacts, there are strong disagreements at home and abroad as to the best course for dealing with the issue. Further complicating the international scene, as reflected in the Kyoto Protocol, is the sharp split between the views of the developing countries, which are reluctant to commit any funds to addressing the issue, and many of the developed countries, which believe early action by all countries is warranted.

Given the central role of the Department in addressing this topic in Washington, in capitals around the world, and at international negotiations, the need for many Department officers to have a high level of familiarity with the scientific as well as the political issues is clear.

An International Protocol to Regulate Genetically Modified Organisms

The 1993 Convention on Biological Diversity calls for an international agreement on biosafety directed to international trade and transfer of life forms altered by bioengineering techniques. The United States has not ratified the Convention, which has been ratified or accepted by 175 countries, and therefore the United State can participate in but cannot vote at negotiations for the new agreement called the Biosafety Protocol. The United States produces about 80 percent of the world's goods and commodities that involve biotechnology, including increased agricultural exports now valued at $60 billion annually.

The U.S. Government supports a Biosafety Protocol that would protect plants and animals from threats posed by living modified organisms but believes the proposed protocol goes well beyond such concerns and could disrupt trade. Among the requirements that the United States considers unacceptable are (1) broad new labeling requirements for consumer products and commodities that are not released into the environment and (2) import permits on a case-by-case basis for bioengineered products that cross international borders. In 1999, the United States mobilized the support of six agricultural exporting nations in blocking efforts to reach agreement on a Biosafety Protocol with such requirements.

In retrospect, the Department of State could have used the resources of the STH community to encourage the development of a Biosafety Protocol that is more consistent with U.S. foreign policy objectives. First, in 1992, greater attention to

Box 1-1 Continued

the implications of the provisions of the Convention on Biological Diversity might have led to a more appropriate formulation concerning the scope of the Biosafety Protocol. Second, development of an international scientific consensus on the technical aspects of genetically modified organisms would have contributed to a better-informed dialogue at the international negotiations.

Arsenic in Drinking Water Wells in Bangladesh

Beginning in the late 1960s, almost 4 million wells were drilled in Bangladesh to solve the drinking water problem—financed by both bilateral and multilateral foreign assistance organizations. In the early 1980s, arsenic was discovered to be contaminating a large number of the wells—perhaps 50 percent. However, no remedial action was seriously considered until the 1990s. Now the World Bank and several European countries are attempting to reverse what has been characterized as the largest case of mass poisoning in the world.

World Bank officials have attributed the problem to a lack of science and technology competence within the Bangladeshi government. At the same time, the many development agencies that have been involved cannot be excused for this serious lack of attention to arsenic poisoning. The U.S. Government, with its sophisticated water quality assessment capabilities and its long-standing assistance efforts in Bangladesh, must of course share the blame.

Anxieties Concerning Plague Outbreak

In 1994, Indian health authorities reported an outbreak of plague in Surat and in a rural area near Bombay. These reports triggered embargoes on travelers from the Middle East and imports of certain commodities.

The U.S. Embassy in New Delhi offered to provide expert investigators from the Centers for Disease Control and Prevention, but the Indians declined the offer. The U.S. Ambassador then called in investigators anyway to check on the conditions being encountered by American diplomats. Once investigators were on the scene, the Indians agreed to accept their assistance as long as they were identified as specialists from the World Health Organization (WHO) Collaborating Center for Plague in Atlanta and were joined by specialists from other countries. By the time the investigators were finally on the scene, the outbreak had subsided; the team issued public health guidelines, and the WHO declared an end to the emergency. The embargoes were then lifted.

The incident underscored the importance of the Department working closely with other U.S. departments and agencies and with international organizations. The Science Officer in New Delhi, a specialist in health affairs, was particularly effective in this regard. Also, it highlighted the sensitivity of STH-related developments that very directly affect the lives of people.

Protection of Scientific Databases

Commercial firms have made significant investments in developing the computer software for cataloging, storing, and retrieving large quantities of data, including scientific research data. Naturally, these companies want to protect these developments by obtaining intellectual property rights to them, while the scientific community wants to minimize any barriers to the exchange and use of research data.

In 1997, the World Intellectual Property Organization considered a proposal for according property rights to the developers of scientific databases who could then market access to the data at rates they considered appropriate. On the eve of the negotiations, the U.S. scientific community became aware of this agenda item and persuaded the U.S. Government to oppose a legal framework that would inappropriately inhibit access by researchers to scientific data.

This incident involving late intervention by leading American scientific institutions was an example of the breakdown in coordination between the Office of Patents and Trademarks, the Office of the U.S. Trade Representative, the Department, and the scientific community.

STH and the Summit of the Americas

Ten of the 23 initiatives adopted at the 1994 Summit of the Americas in Miami call for significant involvement of the STH communities in cooperative efforts throughout the hemisphere. In addition, the 1998 Summit Plan of Action adopted in Santiago emphasizes the importance of cooperation in health technologies, climate change, telecommunications, mitigation of damage from natural disasters, the role of small- and medium-sized innovative companies, and science and technology in general. These documents provide a framework for the programs financed by the Inter-American Development Bank and the Organization of American States.

The United States played a leading role in developing these documents. Although the career Foreign Service Officer with responsibility for developing and presenting the U.S. position had little background in STH-related issues, he skillfully mobilized the capabilities of many U.S. departments and agencies to support his effort. Then, with the assistance of the Office of Science and Technology Policy, he shaped an agenda that was received enthusiastically by Latin American governments.

Terrorism and Forensics

The terrorist bombings of the World Trade Center in New York, a U.S. Air Force housing complex in Saudi Arabia, and U.S. embassies in Kenya and Tanzania have dramatically increased the attention of the Department and other departments and agencies to terrorist threats. A critical aspect of the U.S. response to such incidents is a strong commitment to find and punish the perpetrators. The Department believes that each forensic success followed by apprehension and prosecution will help deter future terrorist attacks.

Although the Federal Bureau of Investigation, Central Intelligence Agency, Department of Defense, and other departments and agencies have the technical capabilities for investigating terrorist incidents, the Department plays a key leadership and facilitating role in Washington and abroad. The Department coordinates the activities of the Technical Working Group involving 40 departments and agencies that supports development of new technological capabilities to combat terrorism, while ambassadors and staffs in the countries of concern provide an essential interface with local authorities both during the immediate response to incidents and during subsequent investigations. Since terrorist attacks could occur in almost every country, the importance of FSOs and other Department officials having a familiarity with the forensic sciences as applied to terrorism is clear.

At the same time, American specialists are a cornerstone of the international STH communities, communities that share a common culture across national borders and are thus themselves a force in the conduct of foreign policy. Shared concerns are reflected, for example, in a large number of bilateral STH cooperative agreements, an expanding array of multilateral arrangements that promote large numbers of research projects, evolving multilateral regimes that help limit the worldwide spread of dangerous materials and technologies, and international responses to many types of problems that threaten the long-term security of populations throughout the world. The development of such international arrangements that facilitate the initiation and implementation of STH programs and of those that constrain harmful and dangerous activities is of high priority. (Table 1-1 and Figure 1-1, exemplifying the international reach of the American STH community, portray technology exports and scientific publications authored jointly by researchers from different countries.) In all of these areas, the Department can play a key

TABLE 1-1   Increase in Internationally Coauthored Scientific and Technical Articles

Country of Author	All Articles with Authors from the Country[a]		Internationally Coauthored (% of total)	
	1981	1995	1981	1995
United States	132,278	142,792	8	19
United Kingdom[b]	30,794	32,980	13	29
Former USSR states	29,610	21,749	3	26
Germany	26,837	30,654	14	33
Japan	25,088	39,498	5	14
France	18,567	23,811	15	34
Canada	14,440	17,359	17	31
India	11,725	7,851	5	15
Italy	7,803	14,117	16	35
Netherlands	5,993	9,239	17	35
Sweden	5,846	7,190	18	39
Switzerland	4,801	5,896	27	48
Israel	3,698	4,322	22	37
China	1,100	6,200	13	29

[a]Data include all scientific and technical articles in natural science and engineering fields.
[b]Data for Hong Kong are included with United Kingdom in 1981.

SOURCES: Institute for Scientific Information, Science Citation Index; CHI Research, Inc., Science Indicators database; and National Science Foundation, unpublished tabulations.

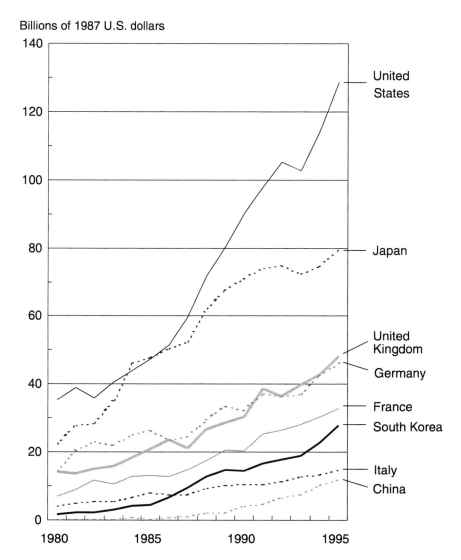

FIGURE 1-1   High-tech exports. SOURCE: Appendix Table 6-5, *Science and Engineering Indicators—1998*, National Science Foundation.

role in promoting political and economic objectives of the U.S. Government that encompass interests of the American STH communities.

Precisely because STH developments are a pervasive global force, they cannot be isolated from the fundamental workings of foreign policy, and effective foreign policy must reflect a comprehensive approach within the Department to integrating STH competence into policy and program formulation and execution.

INADEQUACY OF THE U.S. RESPONSE TO THE
STH CHALLENGE

Since the 1950s, technically trained personnel in specialized offices within the Department have addressed many aspects of STH that impinge on foreign policy and have assisted many departments and agencies, industry, academia, and other nongovernmental organizations in conducting international STH programs. For a short period 40 years ago, there was a Science Advisor to the Secretary; at other times "science" has been included in the title of an undersecretary, reflecting a special responsibility in this area. Since 1974, an assistant secretary, serving as the Director of OES, has been a focal point for many civilian-oriented STH activities (see Box 1-2), while other bureaus have led efforts concerning STH-related issues with significant military or economic aspects. Of special relevance is the recent absorption by the Department of the responsibilities and staff of ACDA, including more than 100 specialists with high levels of technical skills. Additional units of the Department play important roles in handling STH issues of interest to international organizations and to the U.S. intelligence community.

STH developments are of considerable importance at many U.S. embassies and missions to international organizations. More than 200 Department positions overseas are designated to deal with STH-related matters on either a full- or a part-time basis as of July 1999, as discussed in

---

BOX 1-2
Bureau of Oceans and International Environmental and
Scientific Affairs

SEC. 9 (a) There is established within the Department of State a Bureau of Oceans and International Environmental and Scientific Affairs. There shall be an Assistant Secretary of State for Oceans and International Environmental and Scientific Affairs, appointed by the President, by and with the advice and consent of the Senate, who shall be the head of the Bureau and who shall have responsibility for matters relating to oceans, environmental, scientific, fisheries, wildlife, and conservation affairs and for such other related duties as the Secretary may from time to time designate.

SOURCE: Excerpted from the Department of State Appropriations Authorization Act of 1973 (P.L. 93-126; 87 Stat. 453)

Chapter 4 of this report. In addition, many FSNs (i.e., foreign nationals serving as embassy employees) also support such activities.

FSOs occupy many of the most important policy positions within the Department, including a number that are heavily engaged in dealing with STH-related issues. FSOs occupy almost all overseas positions designated as STH positions. At the same time, most FSOs are much more adept at handling political, economic, consular, public diplomacy, and administrative issues than grappling with complex STH topics that do not match their backgrounds.

Also, political appointees, civil servants, and specialists assigned from other departments and agencies play significant roles in addressing STH-related issues. Some of these officials have strong educational backgrounds and extensive experience relevant to their STH responsibilities, but others do not. Some fully appreciate the foreign policy considerations surrounding STH developments, whereas others are weak in this area.

For more than two decades, the Foreign Service Institute (FSI) has been aware of the need for focused efforts to acquaint FSOs and other Department personnel with STH developments of special relevance to foreign policy. Many short courses have been offered on various aspects of STH, and STH developments are increasingly covered as minor elements in longer-term courses for both junior and senior FSOs. However, FSI has considerable difficulty attracting key personnel to participate in specialized STH training since such personnel usually are fully occupied with operational responsibilities, and it is not easy to arrange their release for training assignments. The striking difference between the hesitant attitudes toward training within the Department and the enthusiastic support for training prevalent in industry and the military is discussed in Chapter 3.

Despite the commitment by the Department of many positions to STH activities, the recruitment of technical talent by a number of offices of the Department, and training programs initiated by FSI to upgrade STH competence, **the Department's record in integrating STH capabilities into the development and implementation of foreign policy has not been commensurate with the growing importance of foreign policy issues with STH content.** This reality is reflected in the request of the Secretary for this study and in comments to the committee by dozens of well-informed observers from within and outside the Department. The record of integration is stronger in some areas (e.g., military affairs, arms control, environmental diplomacy) than others (e.g., basic science, global industrial interests, nonnuclear energy). Yet even in the areas of greatest strength, there are gaps in capabilities, and efforts to use technical talent that is available within and outside the U.S. Government have been uneven. Too often, STH considerations are considered simply as minor appendages to foreign policy discussions, and many international STH programs are handled as a special category of activities only vaguely related to the implementation of U.S. foreign policy. The lack of a stronger commitment by the Department to bringing STH considerations into the mainstream of foreign policy formulation and implementation may result in the loss of specific opportunities to take advantage of America's extensive STH capabilities.

At present, STH competence does not receive recognition as an important aspect of the culture of the Foreign Service, a shortcoming that is reflected in several ways:

• STH activities are not high on the agendas of senior Department officials, nor does STH competence weigh heavy during recruitment, training, assignment, and promotion of FSOs. Thus, with occasional exceptions, the most highly talented FSOs are ill equipped for and have little incentive to seek assignments in STH-related positions.

• Many senior Department officers have little motivation to pay attention to STH-related issues, which may require delving into unfamiliar technical content with limited personal rewards for successful mastery of complex issues. This attitude at senior levels sends an important signal to more junior officers that the STH content of issues is not important.

• International STH programs of interest to other departments and agencies and to the private sector often receive low priority within the Department. The Department's primary focus on immediate political, economic, and security issues, important as they may be, frequently results in delays in launching STH programs with potential political as well as technical payoffs for the United States.

Stimulating greater interest in STH should be high on the Department's agenda in responding to the demands of modern diplomacy.

ADJUSTING TO THE CHANGING DIPLOMATIC AGENDA

As STH developments become an ever more critical factor in shaping future U.S. relations with many countries and in offering opportunities for global leadership by the United States, the Department needs to build on existing capabilities and develop a more concerted approach for drawing on external STH resources, specifically:

• The Secretary and other senior officials, with the assistance of their staffs, should know when to seek advice on the STH aspects of important issues, how to frame key questions, and how to identify critical emerging

STH-related issues and important technical uncertainties for consideration by STH experts. STH advice must be presented to these officials in an understandable form and must be meaningful within a foreign policy context.

• All FSOs, as well as other Department officials with foreign policy responsibilities, need a high level of sensitivity in recognizing the importance and relevance of STH-related issues. They should know where to turn within the Department, other departments and agencies, or elsewhere to obtain authoritative information for addressing technical issues.

• The Department needs in-house clusters of STH expertise that can respond promptly to complicated queries and can help frame technical issues when external advice is needed. These in-house staffs should be skilled in identifying emerging issues. Also, they should be able to translate technical advice into contexts and language familiar within the Department and to present advice in ways that will trigger appropriate action.

• Strengthened U.S. embassy staffs should help ensure that the work of the embassies reflects a sound appreciation of STH developments that affect bilateral and multilateral relations, should interact effectively with STH officials and other leaders of the local STH communities both to share information and to help facilitate cooperative activities, and should disseminate information to interested U.S. constituencies on STH developments with foreign policy significance.

Achieving these objectives will depend on (1) a higher-level commitment of the Secretary and other senior officials to create a strengthened organizational and policy framework and (2) a motivated and qualified workforce that encourages and facilitates the integration of STH developments with foreign policy formulation and implementation.

THE DEPARTMENT'S EXPERIENCE WITH CROSSCUTTING PROGRAMS

During the past several decades, the Department has created a number of bureaus and programs with activities that cut across the interests of many countries and international organizations. As previously noted, for four decades, science and technology have also been considered as a crosscutting or "functional" program deserving a special organizational home; but when OES was established to serve this purpose, STH considerations already extended across other functional programs as well. Many STH activities have remained within the purview of these other functional areas (e.g., export control), some have gained considerable prominence within the newly established OES (e.g., fisheries), and some simply have been given low priority (e.g., nonnuclear energy developments). During the 1990s, with reductions of the Department's staff and budget, its capability to maintain a strong, *broadly based* STH capability waned. A number of senior officials of the Department have characterized the current lack of recognition within the Department of the importance of STH developments to foreign policy as analogous to the situation with economics several decades ago, well before economic competence was accepted as a cornerstone of U.S. diplomatic efforts.

Past efforts of the Department to elevate the status of economics and of environmental diplomacy within the Department are instructive in two respects. In both cases they succeeded in focusing the immediate attention of the Department on steps to be taken to enhance its performance in these areas. Secondly, they suggest approaches that might help gain greater recognition throughout the Department, and throughout the entire U.S. foreign policy community, of the essential role of STH capability.

Specifically, in 1986, Secretary George Shultz announced the following enhancements to the personnel and management policies of the Foreign Service in response to the growing importance of foreign economic policies and the increasing complexity of international trade and finance issues:

- Establish rigorous, functionally oriented recruitment standards for FSOs assigned to the economic personnel cone.
- Provide increased opportunities for FSOs to gain relevant work experience, especially as junior officers, and increase the number of advanced economic training assignments available to midlevel officers.
- Give the Bureau of Economic and Business Affairs (EB) a significant role in the management of the Foreign Service's economic talent, including recommendations for all midcareer and senior economic positions, both abroad and within the Department.
- Expand opportunities for economic officers to compete for midlevel and senior program management positions, including chief-of-mission assignments.
- Accelerate office automation in EB.[1]

Then in 1996, Secretary Warren Christopher, largely in response to the many global environmental issues being raised within the United States and at international forums around the world, issued a wide-ranging memorandum on "Integrating Environmental Issues into the

---

[1]"Shultz Wants Greater Role for Economics, Economics Officers." *State* no. 292 (August-September 1986): 2-6.

Department's Core Foreign Policy" that set the stage for many policy and administrative actions throughout the Department. This was followed by a more detailed report on those environmental issues and activities that should be of priority concern to the Department. The memorandum, report, and follow-on actions to elaborate policies and to strengthen the personnel capabilities of the Department in the environmental field were watershed events in enhancing the environmental diplomacy efforts of the United States. Two particularly significant implementation steps with both positive and negative consequences were (1) the establishment abroad of environmental hubs that provide reporting and representation functions concerning environmental issues in selected regions of the world and (2) the diversion of personnel positions that had been assigned for work on science and technology cooperation on a broad basis to provide increased staff for more narrowly focused environmental diplomacy activities within the Department.[2]

In sum, the Department has had experience in making organizational adjustments and devoting personnel resources to crosscutting topics that are perceived as deserving greater emphasis. Sometimes, such adjustments are initiated internally, but more often they respond to pressures from Congress or other external forces. The economics and environmental models cited above may provide a good point of departure for a reinvigoration of STH-related efforts on a broad basis. Substantively, STH-related issues are more akin to economics than to environmental concerns in that they touch on so many aspects of foreign policy. They should not be considered simply a concern of a narrowly focused constituency searching for a seat at the foreign policy table but rather should be of keen interest to all participants in the foreign policy process.

DRAWING ON THE STH STRENGTHS OF THE UNITED STATES

America's capabilities in STH are among the nation's strongest assets in promoting a foreign policy that will create a more secure, prosperous, and democratic world for the benefit of the American people. Individual genius and American entrepreneurship have led to a period of unrivaled technology-driven economic growth within the United States. Many of the world's best scientists and engineers, as well as tens of thousands of

---

[2]Warren Christopher, "Memorandum to All Under and Assistant Secretaries: Integrating Environment Issues into the Department's Core Foreign Policy Goals," February 14, 1996; Bureau of Oceans and International Environmental and Scientific Affairs, *Environmental Diplomacy: The Environment and U.S. Foreign Policy*, Department of State Publication 10470, April 1997.

STH-oriented foreign students, continue to move to the United States for temporary or permanent residence each year. Thus, for the foreseeable future, with the United States using both its native human resources and expertise from abroad, American science and technology will continue to be a pacesetter for the world.

The Department is in an excellent position to draw on the capabilities of the U.S. STH community to obtain authoritative information and considered advice on complex issues such as limitations on rocket technologies, health and environmental implications of trade in genetically modified food products, and the potential of new types of energy sources. Moreover, the Department has the opportunity to promote new international STH programs—in space, on the oceans, in laboratories, and elsewhere—that serve the mutual interests of the United States and partner countries. Also, the Department can call on the STH communities to provide early warning and suggested policies on major issues that affect many nations, such as those whose population growth rates are high, food supplies constrained, and land and water resources overtaxed.

In sum, the nation's foreign policy agenda is constantly facing new challenges, many driven by STH developments at home and abroad; but the culture of the Foreign Service, the Department, and indeed the foreign affairs community in general places relatively low value on STH skills. Although the Department can draw on the extensive STH resources of the country, there must be greater STH awareness throughout the Department and adequate mechanisms within it for utilizing external STH resources in a timely and effective manner. Success in the development of skills to handle issues with STH content by employees throughout the Department will be a significant determinant of how U.S. foreign policy benefits from STH advances that have propelled American economic and national security capabilities to the forefront and have made American science the envy of the world.

2

Leadership Within the Department of State for Addressing STH-Related Issues

THE POLICY FRAMEWORK

The responsibilities for STH-related issues within the Department are spread among many bureaus and offices. The diffuse nature of these responsibilities is both inevitable, in view of the pervasiveness of the issues, and appropriate, given the importance of ensuring that STH considerations are on the agendas of decision-makers throughout the Department. At the same time, this spread of responsibilities and capabilities requires special efforts to help ensure consistency and synergism in addressing related issues that may involve many organizations at home and abroad that deal with multiple offices of the Department and different sections of embassies on such issues.

An essential first step in strengthening STH capabilities within the Department is a clear signal that the Secretary recognizes the significance of such capabilities, the importance of integrating informed STH considerations into foreign policy deliberations, and the need to strengthen STH capabilities. Also, the Secretary must demonstrate a commitment to taking steps to improve the Department's performance in carrying out its responsibilities that involve STH considerations. Thus, the first recommendation is critical and serves as the basis for the committee's further recommendations.

Recommendation: *The Secretary should articulate and implement a policy that calls for greater attention to the STH dimensions of foreign policy throughout the Department and provides guidance as to* *sources of STH expertise available to Department officials in Washington and abroad.*

To be meaningful and have lasting impact, the policy statement should be but the starting point for developing an expanded vision among the Department's leadership as to how STH developments of both longstanding and emerging interest can be brought more fully into the foreign policy process. The Secretary should ensure that such a policy statement is regularly updated and widely disseminated both in Washington and to the embassies and missions abroad. The policy statement and the expanded vision should be accompanied by an action agenda that includes the steps recommended in this report, particularly those designed to enhance Department-wide STH competence in the long term. Implementation of these recommendations should proceed simultaneously on parallel but related tracks. Meanwhile, the Department should continue its efforts to incorporate the STH elements of foreign policy issues and their implications more fully into its strategic planning process, at both the Departmental and the country team levels, reaching out to governmental and nongovernmental STH communities for suggestions concerning the incorporation of STH-related goals into the planning process and proposals for achieving these goals.

STRENGTHENING THE ORGANIZATIONAL STRUCTURE

The Department's leadership (the "Seventh Floor") addresses STH-related issues primarily when an international crisis arises (e.g., an Ebola threat), a contentious and/or important international meeting is approaching (e.g., global climate change negotiations, meeting of a bilateral vice-presidential-level commission), or a country of concern ventures into questionable STH activities (e.g., Iranian interest in nuclear and biological technologies in Russia). There are not adequate mechanisms rooted on the Seventh Floor to accomplish the following:

• Ensure that significant STH-content issues of near-term concern, and particularly those that cross bureau lines of responsibility such as energy issues, are receiving adequate scientific and policy attention involving all interested components of the Department.
• Identify and analyze STH-content issues on the horizon and provide alternative policy options for addressing these issues, with special attention to issues that evolve slowly and are not directly linked to ongoing high-priority policy debates, such as the implications of demographic trends and of water shortages in ecologically sensitive areas of the world.
• Ensure awareness within appropriate offices of significant interna-

tional activities of other U.S. organizations with relevance to foreign policy, including other departments and agencies, U.S.-based companies, scientific institutions, and nongovernmental organizations.

Although organizational adjustments will not in and of themselves ensure better and more timely policies, establishment of clear responsibilities can help avoid neglect and bureaucratic deadlock. Thus, the committee has developed several organizational recommendations to improve the Department's capabilities to address the foregoing concerns.

> **Recommendation:** *The Secretary should provide continuing leadership that ensures consideration within the Department of the STH aspects of issues. To this end, the Secretary should delegate to an undersecretary responsibility for ensuring consideration of STH factors in policy formulation, especially during meetings and consultations involving the Secretary and/or the Secretary's senior advisors and during day-to-day activities at all levels of the Department. The title of the selected undersecretary should be amended to include the phrase "for Scientific Affairs," reflecting the new authority and responsibilities across a broad spectrum of STH aspects of foreign policy.*

The Secretary should make it clear that the oversight responsibilities of the undersecretary extend across the entire Department and involve coordinating the various clusters of STH expertise in the Department to provide an integrated approach to STH matters. The Undersecretary for Global Affairs currently has such responsibilities and should have the title of Undersecretary for Scientific and Global Affairs. Future Secretaries, however, might consider that another undersecretary is the most appropriate official for assuming oversight responsibilities for STH activities.

The undersecretary in the first instance should of course be confident that the bureaus for which he or she is responsible adequately recognize the significance of STH in foreign policy and the importance of policies that facilitate international STH activities. The undersecretary should work with other undersecretaries and assistant secretaries, including those responsible for activities within the geographic bureaus and embassies and missions abroad, to help embed needed STH capabilities and sensitivities throughout the Departmental structure. Also, the undersecretary should collaborate with the Director General of the Foreign Service and the Director of Personnel in providing appropriate career opportunities and incentives for FSOs, civil servants, and other categories of personnel who can bring STH competence to bear within the Department.

Recommendation: *The Secretary should select a highly qualified STH Senior Advisor to the Secretary and to the selected undersecretary to provide expert advice, drawing on the resources of the American STH community as necessary, on current and emerging issues.*

The STH Senior Advisor, with a rank and title appropriate for his or her responsibilities and an adequate staff, should be housed in the office of the undersecretary and should work with senior officials throughout the Department in identifying and addressing important policy and personnel issues and in mobilizing external STH support when necessary. The Senior Advisor should play a particularly significant role in highlighting uncertainties in current issues that should be addressed by STH experts and in identifying emerging issues with important STH dimensions. He or she should report on a day-to-day basis to the undersecretary but should also have a direct reporting relationship to the Secretary. This relationship would enable the Senior Advisor to communicate with the Secretary as appropriate and to take on assignments directly from the Secretary. The Senior Advisor should also serve as the Executive Director of the STH Advisory Committee to the Secretary discussed below.[1]

Operationally, the Senior Advisor should share with the undersecretary responsibilities for addressing organizational and personnel issues as well as other important aspects of developing STH competence within the Department set forth in this report. The Senior Advisor should have important liaison responsibilities with a variety of STH-related institutions both to keep them apprised of relevant developments within the Department and to ensure that their perspectives on foreign policy issues are brought to the attention of responsible Department officials. Should the Department expect the Senior Advisor to participate in international negotiations or otherwise represent it in meetings with foreign officials, he or she should be accorded the rank of Ambassador. Also, at the discretion of the Secretary, he or she might represent the Department in discussions with Congress on complex STH-related issues.

---

[1]The committee is pleased to note that the GS-15 post of Science Advisor previously proposed by the Department is being replaced by a higher level, though as yet unspecified, position. The rank of the Senior Advisor should be at the highest civil service level (SES-6 or GS-18). At the outset, the staff should include a minimum of three professional positions in addition to the Senior Advisor, with the future staff size and composition depending on the evolving responsibilities of the Senior Advisor. The Department has had many dual reporting arrangements over the years with the effectiveness of such arrangements usually dependent on the competence and effectiveness in operating in a large organization of the more junior official. At present, for example, assistant secretaries have direct reporting responsibilities to the Secretary while at the same time serving under the general purview of undersecretaries.

The Senior Advisor should have strong STH credentials through education and/or experience and should be familiar with the governmental, industrial, and academic STH infrastructure of the nation. The Senior Advisor should also have considerable international experience and the capability to integrate STH developments and foreign policy concerns within the Department's policy process.

> **Recommendation:** *The Department should adopt the most appropriate organizational structure for the relevant bureaus and offices in order to meet its STH responsibilities. If legislation is necessary to accomplish this, the Department should seek congressional authorization.*

The current structure is inadequate for the task as reflected in the unattended challenges highlighted in this report. The roles, responsibilities, and capabilities of the undersecretaries and assistant secretaries should be the focal point of a departmental review as the first step in implementing this recommendation. Implementation of the recommendations contained in this report will require adjustments in resource allocations and procedures that probably could be addressed more effectively with a modified organizational structure at the bureau level. An important objective in considering a realignment of operational responsibilities should be the establishment of well-engrained responsibilities for a broad range of STH activities in order to protect against the vagaries of the budget, the priorities of the day, and the special interests of individual officials, which in the past have hindered program stability (e.g., the narrowing of the focus of STH resources within OES to support environmental diplomacy activities). Another objective is to ensure that issues that have not received adequate attention are brought more fully into the mainstream of foreign policy, perhaps through a bureau dedicated to such issues, and not simply considered as additional duties for assistant secretaries preoccupied with environmental or economic concerns (e.g., health, energy, and industrial competitiveness issues). In assessing the organizational options, the Department should continue to seek inputs from the STH community, particularly with regard to the current responsibilities of OES (see Appendix I).

> **Recommendation:** *The Department should establish an STH Advisory Committee to the Secretary and take other steps to further expand the roster of external experts actively engaged in advising the Department's leadership on emerging STH-related issues.*

An advisory committee would provide important continuity as well as a wide range of expertise on emerging major issues, as the Defense

Science Board has done successfully over the years. The purpose of the committee is to enhance the overall capability of the Department and not simply to provide a narrowly focused advocacy forum for the STH community. To this end, the Department should ensure that the committee meets regularly with senior Department officials, including the Secretary, on issues of importance. Given the history of previous scientific advisory committees having had little impact, this new committee should have clear ground rules concerning its functions, authority, and membership. Funds for the committee's activities should be earmarked in the Department's budget. Also, the committee should prepare annual reports for the Secretary and other senior Department officials highlighting conclusions on specific issues that it has addressed. This committee should take into account the activities of other more specialized committees that exist in the national security and economic areas. Other external advisory mechanisms that also should be considered include (1) preparation of an expanded list of consultants who are kept current on STH issues of interest to the Department and who are called upon frequently and (2) tasking of U.S. organizations outside the government to mobilize expertise on selected topics as needed.

RESOURCE REQUIREMENTS

Recommendation: *The Department should increase the resources available to meet the essential STH-related requirements that are recommended in this report.*

The committee's interim report of September 1998 called for allocation of about a dozen new positions to expand STH-related activities in OES, S/P, and INR, and $500,000 annually to begin to support external advisory activities.[2] In addition, adequate resources to support the STH Senior Advisor and a well-qualified staff are essential. Should major structural changes within the Department be required to meet future STH responsibilities, further resources will be needed.

The recommendations in the interim report together with the recommendation for a Senior Advisor and adequate staff are the committee's first priority for additional resource allocations. The second priority of the committee is the additional resources needed to support 25 Science Counselor positions in U.S. embassies and missions, with all of these

---

[2]The current sizes of the units are as follows: OES, 131 staff positions plus 29 in personnel categories not counting against personnel ceilings; S/P, 16 positions; INR, approximately 260 positions, of which about 130 are analysts.

positions to be filled by technically trained specialists with experience in dealing with international STH activities (see Chapter 4). The committee believes that most of the Science Counselor positions could be absorbed within current allocations for overseas science positions, although a number of the existing positions would have to be elevated in rank. The committee's third priority is to provide resources to support major structural changes that might result from the Department's review of the organization of operational STH responsibilities.

Returning to the STH needs of specific offices, several activities warrant special ambassadors who have unusual skills and experience and also time to carry out protracted negotiations and to coordinate activities in Washington. At present, there are special envoys with strong STH credentials for addressing (1) nuclear and related problems in North Korea and (2) nuclear and missile-related transfers from Russia to Iran. In the past, the Bureau of Political-Military Affairs (PM) also has had a special ambassador for nuclear issues, and consideration should be given to reviving this position, given the heightened concern within international agencies as well as the United States over proliferation of nuclear materials and technologies. Within OES, in either its current or future form, one or more special ambassadors designated to lead global environmental negotiations could take a great travel burden off the OES leadership while ensuring that specific topics, such as global climate change and biodiversity, receive sufficient attention on a sustained basis. In a third area, a special negotiator for chemical and biological weapons issues has been nominated with the rank of Ambassador but has not yet been approved

The Department has strong analytical capabilities in the political and economic areas but not in STH-related areas. S/P and INR should develop the capabilities to identify and include STH-related issues in their work so as to enhance the Department's overall capability to integrate STH into the policy process. However, as recommended in the interim report, each will need one or more senior specialists with technical backgrounds to identify STH issues that should receive attention and to raise questions concerning policy responses to such developments.

Two other important bureaus in the Department that are faced with major STH concerns on a daily basis are EB and the Bureau of International Organization Affairs (IO). IO is the Department's principal link with the United Nations and its associated agencies, many of which have significant STH responsibilities. These bureaus have developed mechanisms for supplementing their staff capabilities with expertise available from industry and other departments and agencies. In some cases they could benefit from a broader base of internal and/or external expertise that would not be biased toward special interests, but in general they are relatively well equipped for carrying out their responsibilities.

THE EXTERNAL CONSTITUENCIES

Successful integration of STH developments and foreign policy objectives can provide potent arguments for mobilizing greater support for the international affairs activities of the U.S. Government, particularly from Congress. Unfortunately, in its relationships with Congress, the Department has not fully articulated the benefits for the American people from international STH activities and the critical role of the Department in supporting such activities. The significance of disease prevention, food safety, environmental protection, and nuclear security, for example, is easily understood, and Congress should be quite receptive to expanded efforts in these areas given the number of congressional committees that have international STH developments within their purviews (see Table 2-1). The Assistant Secretary for Public Affairs is in a good position to help improve public understanding on Capitol Hill and throughout the nation of the importance of the STH aspects of foreign policy issues and international programs for the well-being of American citizens.

There are many opportunities for the Department's public diplomacy and educational exchange programs (formerly under USIA) to highlight

TABLE 2-1   Selected Congressional Committees with Interests at the Intersection of Science and Technology with International Affairs

House	Senate
Agriculture	Agriculture, Nutrition, and Forestry
Appropriations	Appropriations
Armed Services	Armed Services
Banking, Housing, and Urban Affairs	Banking, Housing, and Urban Affairs
Budget	Budget
Energy and Commerce	Commerce, Science, and Transportation
Foreign Affairs	Energy and Natural Resources
Intelligence	Environment and Public Works
Science	Foreign Relations
	Intelligence
	Health, Education, Labor, and Pensions

SOURCE: *Science and Technology in U.S. International Affairs*, Carnegie Commission on Science, Technology, and Government, January 1992, p. 19 (modified to reflect committee name changes as of September 1999).

U.S. government-sponsored initiatives in fields such as AIDS prevention and biodiversity conservation. The Undersecretary for Public Diplomacy has access to many resources within and outside the Department, particularly the international networks of scientists that are well known to OES, to improve international understanding of the importance of STH-related issues for global peace and prosperity. Such efforts could readily build on the many contacts at home and abroad developed over decades by USIA, particularly linkages with nongovernmental organizations.

Thousands of American private-sector institutions have strong international STH interests: universities, research institutions, professional societies, health care providers and insurers, manufacturing companies, trading organizations, consulting firms, financial institutions, service companies, charitable groups, and other nongovernmental organizations. Some of their programs are supported financially by other departments and agencies. For others, the U.S. Government may provide introductions abroad, timely advisory services, or authoritative information. Such dependence on the government usually leads to considerable interaction between the organizations and government officials. However, many private activities have no government involvement, and often the government is not even aware that such activities are underway.

International cooperation has for decades been a way of life in most areas of scientific research. Many scientists have long been international travelers, spending time in the laboratories of foreign colleagues and hosting foreign visitors in the United States. Both personal and electronic networks of scientists from a variety of countries working on the same array of problems have become commonplace. Some networks have been established within the framework of formally organized international programs, but most are quite informal, having been initiated by individual scientists who appreciate the payoff from transnational contacts. The payoff can be substantial: for example, of the 147 Nobel Prizes awarded in physics, chemistry, and physiology or medicine since 1950, 60 were given as joint international awards shared by a total of 148 researchers from many countries.[3]

Meanwhile, private companies are expanding their international reach. As a result of international mergers, it becomes more difficult to characterize many companies as American or some other nationality. Multinational companies have moved beyond only searching for emerging markets, new sources of raw materials, and low-cost production opportunities in expanding this global reach. More U.S. companies are

---

[3]See http://www.nobel.se/prize/index.html.

BOX 2-1
Examples of Foreign Policy Issues of Concern to U.S. Industry

- Restrictions on sales of space launch technologies to China
- Impact on commercial relations of allegations of Chinese acquisition of nuclear secrets
- Proposed limitations on the use of global positioning system technology in certain parts of the world
- Proposed restrictions on sales of encryption technology
- Consequences of nuclear testing in India and Pakistan on foreign investment in those countries
- Details of international agreements on intellectual property rights
- Environmental impact of global climatic change and economic consequences of proposed measures to reduce this impact
- Implications of international corporate mergers in the petroleum, telecommunications, and automobile industries
- Implications for U.S. economic and security interests of growth in foreign high-tech R&D investments

SOURCE: Mary L. Good, "Trouble at State," Speech delivered at the Annual Meeting of the American Association for the Advancement of Science, Anaheim, California, January 23, 1999.

---

providing funding for research conducted abroad, while foreign companies are increasingly establishing laboratories in the United States. Thus, it is not surprising that U.S. industry is interested in many issues of priority concern to the Department and also in issues that, while not currently on the Department's agenda, will have significant impacts on international operations in future years.

The economic dimensions of STH developments are manifold. Many near-term consequences of STH-related foreign policy decisions are clearly recognized by U.S. industry, as indicated in Box 2-1. Also, in the longer term, for example, trade relationships can be stimulated through foreign assistance programs. International geological programs can clarify the resource potential of remote regions. Cooperation in developing better telecommunications systems can improve business opportunities throughout the world.

As the role of the private-sector continues to expand overseas, the Department needs greater outreach capabilities to learn from the insights of others, to take advantage of international contacts and international programs that have been developed by others, and to involve the ever-expanding group of stakeholders in international STH activities in formulating and implementing the foreign policy of the nation. Its effectiveness in meeting these challenges is strongly linked to the level of STH competence throughout the Department.

3

Broadening and Deepening STH Competence Within the Department of State

OVERVIEW

Given the increased number of STH-related issues reaching the diplomatic agenda and the growing complexity of the technical considerations, the Department faces the challenges of broadening and of deepening the STH competence of officials handling STH-related issues. **The need for STH competence in Washington and in embassies and missions can be most realistically met through a deliberate mixed strategy that deploys both a limited number of specialized STH experts in several personnel categories and a large number of FSOs and other "generalists" who have acquired a minimum level of STH competence.** In the long term, the objective should be a broadly based "STH-capable" Department.

This approach emphasizes a large number of officials who can recognize the importance of STH considerations and know when and where to seek expert advice. Such a broadly based appreciation of the relevance of STH developments to foreign policy and the ability to obtain appropriate advice when necessary are preferable to past approaches, which have placed excessive reliance on a relatively small number of STH specialists operating amidst large staffs of FSOs and civil servants with limited STH perspectives. STH-content issues are simply too pervasive to expect that specialists will always be available to recognize or handle them. Indeed, action officers in Washington and overseas (primarily FSOs) will usually be the trip wires that signal the need for mobilizing STH expertise. Of course, specialists with strong technical backgrounds will still be needed throughout the Department and at key embassies and missions, not only to support the generalists but also to assume leadership on particularly complex issues. Furthermore, specialists with strong STH credentials and experience can provide an important interface with the broader STH communities in the United States and abroad.

The following recommendation addresses one crucial aspect of the mixed generalist-specialist strategy:

> **Recommendation:** *The Department's leadership should expect all FSOs and other officials of the Department to achieve a minimum level of STH literacy and awareness relevant to foreign policy while stimulating attention to STH throughout the Department by establishing promotion and career incentives for successful service in STH-related positions.*[1]

This recommendation recognizes that the goal of the mixed strategy will be embraced throughout the Department only if STH competence is widely viewed as a career-enhancing asset (i.e., STH-related assignments are recognized as stepping stones to advancement to senior positions within the Department). Implementation of this recommendation requires a comprehensive approach within the personnel system involving the recruitment, assignment, training, and promotion aspects of the careers of Department officials. Working out the details may be difficult in view of the different categories of personnel positions involved in STH-related activities and the different personnel rules within each category. Also, there may be reservations within the Department about attempting to accommodate special needs to address STH issues when there are also needs for specialized skills and sensitivities related to other issues (e.g., labor concerns). Nevertheless, given the stakes involved, the Department should develop a comprehensive approach for implementing a mixed STH personnel strategy over the long term.

At present, the staffing of positions designated as "STH positions" in Washington and at U.S. embassies and missions to international organizations involves officials with different educational backgrounds, different levels of relevant experience, and different types of job classifications. STH positions are filled by FSOs, Foreign Service Reserve Officers (FSRs),

---

[1]STH literacy as used in this report includes an appreciation of basic STH concepts of importance for international affairs, knowledge of the responsibilities and capabilities of the key institutions that comprise the STH infrastructure of the United States, and familiarity with the principal international organizations and agreements that encompass STH developments at home and abroad.

FSNs, civil service officers, political appointees, rotators from other departments and agencies, detailees from academic institutions and government laboratories, American Association for the Advancement of Science (AAAS) fellows, Presidential Management Interns, part-time government retirees, and probably other categories. A limited number of FSOs and civil servants are trained in one or more areas of STH. Some highly trained civil servants have been recruited from other Departments and agencies, government laboratories, and academic institutions as midlevel officers. Almost all AAAS fellows and some Presidential Management Interns have strong STH competence, although there have been financial limitations on the number of such positions.[2]

This personnel situation has evolved largely by happenstance. Each senior manager responsible for STH-related activities obviously wants to have the best staff that he or she can assemble. The manager attempts to attract the highest-quality and most appropriate talent given personnel ceilings, encumbered positions, financial limitations, and different levels of administrative hassle associated with different types of appointments. As a result, some incumbents handling issues with STH content are very well qualified for their assignments, whereas others are not well suited for dealing with technical issues.

Recruitment and assignment of personnel for STH positions other than FSOs are largely decentralized, with each bureau relying on its own budget, its assigned personnel ceiling, and its space and equipment capabilities to support such positions. Recruitment and assignment of FSOs are centralized; many different bureaus are involved in the assignment process to varying degrees, depending in large measure on the priority that a bureau attaches to recruiting specific FSOs of interest.

The committee supports the concept of drawing on a variety of personnel categories in responding to specialized needs for addressing STH-related issues, a policy being implemented by the Department's Bureau of Personnel. The appropriate balance of categories in any specific office depends on many factors, including the availability of skills within the Foreign Service. However, the Bureau of Personnel is concerned over the current balance in some offices. For example, during the past decade the

---

[2]There probably are about 200 positions in Washington that should be classified as STH related (i.e., the incumbents spend more than 50 percent of their time on STH-related foreign policy issues). Overseas, 57 positions are formally classified as Environment, Science, and Technology (EST) positions, with the bulk of the incumbents' time directed to STH-related issues; an additional 30 or so probably involve more than a half-time commitment to STH issues. Of course, there are far more officials involved on a part-time basis in addressing STH-related issues, numbering about 150, and there are probably 200 or more FSNs involved in STH-related issues.

professional staff of OES has been transformed from 70 percent FSOs to 30 percent FSOs, which in the view of the Bureau of Personnel represents too great a shift. As OES responsibilities in the environmental area increased and the staff expanded, OES hired new civil servants for specialized positions with declining attention to opportunities for FSOs to serve in the bureau. Rotating larger numbers of FSOs through OES would certainly be valuable in diffusing STH experience within the Foreign Service, if the FSOs were appropriately trained to assume their responsibilities within OES.

THE CENTRAL ROLE OF FOREIGN SERVICE OFFICERS

Whether formally classified as political, economic, consular, administrative, or public diplomacy officers, FSOs are increasingly called upon to handle issues laden with STH considerations. Although relatively few are assigned to designated STH positions, many spend considerable time addressing STH-related issues during their careers. To carry out these responsibilities effectively, a minimum level of STH literacy is needed throughout the Foreign Service. At present, few FSOs have strong educational backgrounds in STH disciplines, and of those who do have technical degrees, many have shifted their focus to economics, language specialization, and other skills of greater interest to the Department in recent years. At the same time, most FSOs have impressive capabilities to learn quickly, particularly when faced with operational decisions.

Recruitment

Some junior FSOs have well-honed information technology skills. Others have entered the Foreign Service with a keen awareness of global issues, including the implications of STH factors that are shaping economic, technological, environmental, health, agricultural, and other national and international developments. These are important personal qualifications that will contribute to increased recognition within the Foreign Service of the importance of STH developments. The Department should give greater attention to seeking such skills among new FSOs.

However, current recruitment procedures remain heavily oriented toward specialists in history, economics, international relations, area studies, and other fields that are normally very distant from STH curricula. The FSO examination does not effectively screen applicants for even a minimum level of STH literacy. Questions that discern awareness of contemporary developments in STH, as well as major events in American and world history that have been influenced by STH discoveries and applications, are appropriate for the Foreign Service entrance examination. Surely, new entrants, and indeed all FSOs, should have some familiarity with the agricultural and pharmaceutical implications of recent advances in biotechnology, the environmental and health aspects of increased reliance on fossil fuels, and the capability of the electronic networks that are encircling the globe. The Director General of the Foreign Service could easily draw on the U.S. STH communities for suggestions as to modification of the examination to reflect the impact of such STH developments in international affairs.

Also, the Department could expand its targeted recruitment efforts to include STH departments of universities, national laboratories, and other organizations with concentrations of STH-literate professionals. The recruitment brochures used by the Department to attract applicants for the Foreign Service should give greater attention to the increasing importance of STH and the opportunities to have individuals with these skills apply them in international public service, particularly careers in the Foreign Service.

At the same time, the Department's experiment with more flexible entrance procedures is commendable. The current recruitment effort to fill 25 junior FSO positions with civil servants who are already serving within the government will probably include some new entrants with well-developed STH skills.

Career Opportunities

Once recruited, an FSO with serious STH interests should have the opportunity for a meaningful career that builds on but is not restricted to these interests. Of special importance are opportunities for assignments in STH-related positions and for advancement to the highest ranks of the Foreign Service. Also, there is a need for training and retraining so that STH capacity can be kept current with new developments.

As previously noted, an STH-related assignment is seldom considered by senior Department officials to be a career-enhancing activity for an FSO seeking to rise to the level of Ambassador or Deputy Chief of Mission. Nevertheless, many STH-related issues are intellectually challenging, and assignments to handle these issues can frequently provide opportunities to participate in important international negotiations, an activity that is viewed throughout the Foreign Service as contributing to career development. Some FSOs have willingly accepted, and at times eagerly sought, STH-related assignments, and a few have established strong reputations as highly effective officers in these positions.

Serious setbacks to the perceived importance of STH competence in the Foreign Service occurred with the abolishment of the personnel cone for science and technology specialists and the assignment of FSOs with weak STH backgrounds to almost all of the Science Counselor positions in U.S. embassies and missions to international organizations during the mid-1990s. These actions have sent a strong signal that STH competence is not an important asset for FSOs. Indeed, it may be a handicap in the assignment and promotion systems if the affected FSOs have sacrificed the development of other essential skills such as competence in foreign languages in favor of strengthening personal capabilities to handle STH-related issues.

The committee does not recommend re-establishment of the science and technology cone, which was generally considered within the Department as a compartment for specialists who were outside the mainstream of foreign policy and therefore not serious candidates for senior leadership assignments. Moreover, such a compartmentalized approach could inhibit the diffusion of STH competence throughout the Foreign Service. A practical difficulty was the small size of the science and technology cone, namely, no more than approximately 30 FSOs. Since there were hundreds of FSOs in each of several other cones, only a small percentage of the available promotion slots were open to science and technology specialists. They often felt slighted, while some colleagues in other cones thought the competition among science and technology specialists was not as intense as within their cones. Now, with small cadres of FSOs specializing in diplomatic security, labor affairs, narcotics, and other fields requiring specialized skills, the establishment of many small cones is not considered practical. However, other types of personnel actions that stress the importance of STH skills, including those recommended in this report, are needed in the wake of abolishing the cone. Designation of a well-qualified specialist in the Bureau of Personnel with explicit responsibilities for STH career development could be one useful step in this regard. This specialist should be in a good position to learn from approaches taken by private firms and nonprofit organizations as to policies for specialists operating in generalist-oriented organizations.

Bureaus with special responsibilities for STH-related issues often seek out FSOs with STH backgrounds for specific assignments. However, the bureaus seldom encourage these FSOs to maintain and use their competencies over an extended period. Indeed, the committee received reports of FSOs with significant STH competence being discouraged from remaining in STH-related assignments lest they jeopardize their promotion potential. Furthermore, the bureaus seldom make special efforts to ensure that FSOs who perform well in STH assignments receive attractive follow-on assignments. This approach contrasts with the approaches of several geographic bureaus, which seek to rotate throughout the region over many years a large number of outstanding FSOs with area competence.

Finally, most FSOs aspire to the level of Deputy Chief of Mission or Ambassador, positions that frequently require a level of STH competence. Unfortunately, relatively few FSOs have been seriously engaged with STH-related issues, and they are not in a good position to weigh the relative foreign policy import of STH developments. Therefore, the Department should consider establishing a requirement that each FSO who is en route to a senior position must have experience in addressing STH or other global issues. For example, candidates for Ambassador and Deputy Chief of Mission positions could be required to have completed an assignment handling global issues prior to selection for the most senior positions. This requirement would be a loud and clear signal that such issues, including STH-related issues, are important and have become core concerns of the Department.

High-performing FSOs interested in having STH-oriented careers should have reasonable expectations that they can rise to the ambassadorial level. They, like all FSOs, should begin with a broad exposure to Foreign Service challenges and finish with assignments as Deputy Chiefs of Mission and then Ambassadors. In between, their career paths would have many variations, including both STH and non-STH assignments.

Promotions and Rewards

As indicated in the previous section, a key motivating factor for FSOs to become interested in STH-related assignments is the existence of a personnel system that leads to career rewards for successful service in such posts. A significant indicator to FSOs of the importance of STH competence is the promotion scorecard for FSOs who have served in STH assignments. The outcome of the promotion panels is heavily dependent on the precepts that are prepared for the panels and by the composition of the panels. In both areas the Department should ensure that the importance of STH competence is adequately addressed.

A specific suggestion is that the Director General include representatives of the STH community with broad experience among the "outside members" of selection panels. These outside members could provide perspective on the significance of STH-related achievements and the potential of individual FSOs to address foreign policy issues with STH content in the future. Scientific, engineering, and medical societies are in a good position to identify particularly well-qualified retirees who could commit six weeks to such an assignment.

Directly related to the work of the promotion panels, of course, are the requirements for preparing personnel evaluations. The instructions for preparing such evaluations should include consideration of the achievements of FSOs in identifying and developing responses to long-term problems, including STH-related issues, which are often given short shrift due to the high visibility of near-term crises.

Special awards are also ways to recognize performance. For example, the past practice of giving awards for outstanding environmental, science, and technology reporting is important. However, separate awards should be given for environmental reporting, which is perceived as high priority throughout the Department and often dominates the competitions, and for reporting on other aspects of STH, which may be in need of greater attention.

Training

Many aspects of STH-related issues are not easily understood by FSOs who have not had the benefit of scientific or engineering training. Concepts of scientific uncertainty, for example, are often unfamiliar, and factoring such uncertainty into assessments of foreign policy options is not an easy task for even technically trained and politically attuned specialists. Further, there are large and diverse STH communities in the United States and in most other countries. Although specialists with STH training usually become accustomed to reaching out to colleagues in government and the private sector when seeking information and support relevant to their activities, few FSOs are familiar with the activities and capabilities of these communities, which can be a strong handicap for newcomers to STH activities.

In comparison to training programs of industry and the military services, the Department's programs are quite weak except with regard to language training. Even highly effective programs that are offered may be compromised by management decisions that give low priority to training for FSOs who, in the view of supervisors, are needed to fulfill immediate operational responsibilities. The committee recognized that the Department faces budget constraints that limit the availability of replacements for officers in training. However, there seems to be a general bias within the Foreign Service against specialized training courses on the grounds that FSOs are always learning on the job. Neither of these factors is an acceptable reason for maintaining a less than comprehensive training system for all Department employees, including training in STH subjects. The military services and many companies have greatly reduced their staffs over the last decade but have continued to emphasize training. Also, industry has learned that on-the-job training, while important, is not adequate in many respects, particularly with regard to opportunities for midlevel managers to interact with top management in informal settings. This experience should serve as a guide for the Department.

FSI has good capabilities to provide STH-related training for FSOs—

as supplemental modules for broader training programs and as intensive courses limited to STH concerns. Training at FSI is usually well organized and offers considerable promise in elevating FSO sensitivity to STH developments. FSI leadership is aware of STH training limitations of the past and is interested in developing a broadened set of offerings, including part-time courses that do not take individuals completely away from their jobs.

The STH content of the A-100 course for all new FSOs, the economics training program, the Deputy Chief of Mission preparatory course, and the Senior Seminar for FSOs picked for top-level assignments could easily be expanded and tailored to stimulate greater interest in STH developments as they interrelate to foreign policy. Courses in fields such as security, terrorism, and foreign assistance also could include appropriate modules on STH considerations. With regard to self-education, FSI could further develop electronic bookmarks and other distance-learning techniques to help FSOs stay abreast of relevant STH developments on a timely basis.

Seminars that bring together Department personnel with explicit STH responsibilities and FSOs who are not serving in STH-oriented assignments could help develop more meaningful communications and cooperative working relationships within the Department. Included in issue-oriented seminars should be personnel from both the regional bureaus and the functional bureaus and offices such as INR and S/P. These seminars should help encourage the bureaus and offices to work together in identifying slowly evolving issues and in considering how they affect bilateral and multilateral diplomacy and programs.

Finally, several universities offer a rich combination of advanced degree study, including political science and STH-related subjects. For a few outstanding FSOs, the opportunity for a semester or year of advanced STH/political science training could prepare them well for senior positions requiring special STH competence. Such extramural training would also send a powerful signal throughout the Department about the value of STH competence.

CIVIL SERVICE OFFICIALS

Civil service personnel fill many key STH-related positions in the Department. Some have been in their positions for 10 or more years and have developed extensive knowledge of the activities for which they are responsible. Others have been recruited recently and bring with them fresh technical perspectives on important issues. Most are in relatively senior positions. In particular, many office director positions are filled by civil servants.

In time, STH-capable FSOs should increasingly be able to assume responsibilities currently handled by civil servants. However, there will be a continuing need for highly specialized civil servants in the years ahead. Appropriate personnel policies are necessary to ensure that civil servants who are particularly well qualified to address STH-related issues also have the opportunity to advance to the senior ranks within the Department and overseas.

Meanwhile, a particular problem is that many civil service personnel remain indefinitely in their positions and thus close off potentially attractive assignments for FSOs interested in STH developments, although most FSOs would require training to be able to handle the responsibilities involved. A second concern is that, due to pressures within the office, civil service officials, like FSOs, are often reluctant to take time off for training to help ensure that they are up to date on developments relevant to their responsibilities.

As civil servants leave their positions through retirement or for other reasons, opening these positions to competition involving both FSOs and non-FSOs would encourage FSOs to look more seriously at career options in STH areas. To be sure that FSOs are not at a disadvantage in these competitions, which usually call for familiarity with technical issues, their STH qualifications could include a three-month training course tailored to the needs of the position with the course customized by FSI. At the same time, non-FSOs seeking these positions should have the opportunity to attend a foreign policy orientation course at FSI if they are selected for the positions so that they too would not be at a disadvantage in the competitions.

A few civil servants, particularly in PM, take advantage of opportunities to stay abreast of developments in their technical fields through participation in programs organized by the Department of Defense and other departments and agencies. This practice is very healthy and should be encouraged throughout the Department. The FSI might give special attention to how such training activities could be most effectively organized and promoted on a broad basis.

An important source of recruitment for civil servants with specialized skills and experience in dealing with foreign policy issues has been the pool of AAAS fellows selected for one-year assignments to the Department, particularly OES. In most cases during their tenure as fellows, they have exhibited a high level of STH competence of relevance to the issues confronting the Department, and they have quickly adjusted to departmental work. In some instances, they have received civil service appointments within the Department and have become important permanent staff members. Given this excellent track record of the program both in providing temporary coverage of important issues and in serving as a recruitment pipeline, the Department, in consultation with the AAAS and other scientific, engineering, and medical organizations, should consider how this type of program could be expanded.

Finally, over the years, ACDA has recruited many highly qualified technical specialists; and a number of these specialists have recently been incorporated into the bureaus under the Undersecretary for Arms Control and International Security. Since these bureaus already had a significant number of technical personnel, there may be technical talent that could be used in other bureaus of the Department.

Some ACDA specialists were recruited under special hiring authority available to the agency. This authority was very important in attracting specialized skills to address critical technical aspects of important arms control issues, and the authority has recently been transferred to the Department. The Department should broadly utilize as necessary the special hiring authority that has been transferred to it from ACDA to recruit highly qualified specialists, generally for terms of one to four years. This authority, together with the other authorities previously available to the Department, provides considerable flexibility for achieving the personnel goals proposed in this report.

INFORMATION TECHNOLOGIES

Modern information technology (IT) systems provide opportunities for broadening and deepening the Department's STH competence as discussed earlier in this chapter. The development of modern IT systems in the Department is essential for the conduct of diplomacy in the years ahead. Modern systems are also essential to the full implementation of many of the recommendations in this report. Obsolete IT systems within the Department and at embassies and missions abroad greatly hamper the efforts of employees to improve productivity, communicate effectively with governmental and nongovernmental organizations, and use Internet resources in many areas, including STH.

The Department has recently developed and begun to implement an impressive five-year plan for upgrading its worldwide IT systems. A highly qualified Chief Information Officer, with the rank of assistant secretary, has been recruited to lead this effort. As an early achievement, he and his staff succeeded in changing the Department's report card prepared by government auditors for year 2000 compliance from an F in February 1999 to an A– by May 1999.[3]

---

[3]See <http://www.house.gov/reform/gmit/y2k/index.htm>.

The Department's IT plan is designed to (1) ensure year 2000 compliance, (2) improve security as necessary, (3) provide Internet access for personnel in the United States and abroad, (4) train users, and (5) put in place a program of continuous improvement and maintenance. OES is being used as an "IT test bed" for prototyping systems and policies. The IT modernization program should ease the integration of USIA and ACDA into the Department because these agencies are at present far better equipped than the Department with up-to-date IT systems and software. Prompt implementation of the IT five-year plan should also improve the job satisfaction of many young Department employees who have grown up in the information age.

Modern IT systems are well suited for facilitating distance learning—a useful approach for FSOs, civil servants, and specialized STH staff who have difficulty committing to specific training schedules but who would like to participate in training programs from remote sites (either in formal programs of FSI and other providers or informally through the Internet). As a stimulus to encourage greater use of this important technology, those FSOs who successfully complete Internet- or other computer-based self-taught training programs in STH fields should be recognized in their personnel evaluations or in other ways.

Also, embassy personnel with STH responsibilities should have ready access to many online STH resources, including information on the reports, activities, and interests of a variety of U.S. departments and agencies with STH interests. In addition, there are vast resources in the published official statistics of many countries, often with useful historical depth, that should be available to FSOs and other analysts at a mouse click.

Institutional reluctance to accept new IT technologies could be a significant barrier to successful implementation of the five-year plan. Some employees, conditioned by Cold War security requirements and a hierarchical diplomatic clearance process developed many years ago, may not be entirely comfortable with the open access and flexibility that modern IT systems provide. A second difficulty that afflicts many long-term government procurement programs will undoubtedly be encountered in sustaining the multiyear IT procurement through cycles of annual appropriations, changes of administration, and changes in Congress. Thus, the following recommendation is particularly important:

Recommendation: *The Secretary, the Administration, and Congress should ensure that the Department's five-year information technology modernization plan stays on course and is fully funded for its successful implementation and also for necessary ongoing maintenance and upgrades.*

There is no better example of the impact of STH developments on the development and implementation of foreign policy than IT systems. Whether they are used to enhance the internal processes of the Department, to expand outreach to constituencies and information sources around the world, or to offer new opportunities for increasing the skill levels of diplomats and other personnel, they are clearly transforming the art of diplomacy and powerfully affecting the international issues nations must confront.

4

STH Expertise at
U.S. Embassies and Missions

OVERVIEW

It is in U.S. embassies and missions to international organizations that much of the melding of the requirements of diplomacy and the contributions of experts takes place. To this end, the assignment of specialized STH personnel to embassies and missions has been an established pattern since 1950. In general, these specialists have been particularly active in five areas:

1. *Alerting embassy and Department officials to emerging problems and opportunities associated with new STH developments in the United States and abroad*: Such anticipatory activities frequently prevent the escalation of problems to crisis levels while identifying opportunities to use STH capabilities to further U.S. interests.

2. *Providing an informed technical perspective during internal embassy deliberations on issues involving significant STH considerations*: STH-related issues vary widely from post to post and frequently dominate embassy agendas, particularly in large and important countries. (Box 4-1 lists some of the topics that are currently important in a number of countries and regions.)

3. *Assisting U.S. departments and agencies during the development and negotiation of bilateral STH agreements and programs and facilitating the implementation of these arrangements*: This responsibility is especially significant

in countries where broad bilateral umbrella agreements provide frameworks for large numbers of programs (e.g., Japan, South Africa, Egypt).

4. *Obtaining and disseminating information concerning (1) changes and other developments in the STH policies of the host government, (2) local STH achievements that are noteworthy, and (3) international STH activities supported by the host government of relevance to U.S. interests*: Such information is particularly useful in countries that retain close control over information sources (e.g., China, Russia).

5. *Providing an informed point of contact for local officials and specialists interested in STH policies, organizations, and technical achievements in the United States*: Countries with growing and vibrant STH communities repeatedly look to the United States for contacts and guidance in STH endeavors (e.g., Israel, Korea, Taiwan, Brazil).

For several decades, many Science Counselors and a number of more junior Science Officers at the embassies were scientists and engineers with advanced STH degrees.[1] Some had extensive laboratory experience, and almost all were well informed about the STH communities in the United States and knowledgeable about the interests of U.S. departments and agencies. They knew where to obtain technical support expeditiously when an issue required specialized expertise that was not available within the embassy.

After a peak of 22 in the 1980s, the number of Science Counselor positions has declined steadily to 10 in 1999,[2] while the number of full-time Science Officer positions (including Science Counselors and environmental hub officers) has increased to 57. Despite this increase, the number of Department officials in embassy and mission Science Officer positions with degrees in science or engineering has shrunk in the past 15 years from more than 25 to about 15.[3] The current distribution of full-time and part-time Science Officers assigned to embassies, totaling more than 200 U.S. diplomats, is set forth in Table 4-1. This large number of

---

[1]Over the years the terminology used for specialists assigned by the Department to the embassies has varied—Science and Technology Counselors; Environmental, Science, and Technology Counselors; Science Attachés; Science Officers; and Environmental Officers, for example. For this report the titles Science Counselors and Science Officers are used to include positions with slightly different names as well.

[2]The estimate of 22 was provided by a former Department official knowledgeable about their activities. More precise information is not readily available from the Department.

[3]The Department provided the committee with partial information suggesting that perhaps 20 percent of these full-time incumbents have undergraduate or graduate degrees in science or engineering (not including political science and other social sciences).

TABLE 4-1 Environment, Science, and Technology (EST) Positions at U.S. Embassies and Missions

Post	Science Counselor[a]	Science Officer	Part-Time Officer	Environmental Hub
Abu Dhabi			1	
Abidjan				1
Abuja			1	
Accra			1	
Adana			1	
Addis Ababa				1
AIT/Kaohsiun			1	
AIT/Taipei		1	1	
Algiers			1	
Almaty			1	
Amman				1
Ankara				1
Antananarivo			1	
Apia			1	
Asuncion			1	
Athens			1	
Auckland			1	
Bamako			1	
Bandar SB			1	
Bangkok				1
Beijing		4		
Beirut			1	
Bern			1	
Bissau			1	
Bogota			1	
Bonn		1	6	
Brasilia				1
Bratislava			1	
Bridgetown			1	
Brussels-US		1	1	
Brussels-NATO	1		1	
Bucharest			1	
Budapest		1		
Buenos Aires	1	1		
Bujumbura			1	
Cairo			2	
Calcutta			1	
Calgary			1	
Canberra			1	
Cape Town			1	
Caracas			2	
Casablanca			1	
Chengdu			1	
Chennai			1	
Chiang Mai			1	
Colombo			1	

TABLE 4-1 Continued

Post	Science Counselor[a]	Science Officer	Part-Time Officer	Environmental Hub
Conakry			1	
Copenhagen				1
Cotonou			1	
Dakar			1	
Damascus			1	
Dar Es Salaam			1	
Dhaka			1	
Dubai			1	
Dublin			1	
Fukuoka			2	
Gaborone			1	
Geneva-USMIS	1			
Georgetown			1	
Guangzhou			1	
Guatemala City			1	
Guayaquil			1	
Hanoi	1			
Harare			1	
Helsinki			1	
Hermosillo			1	
Hong Kong			2	
Islamabad			1	
Istanbul			1	
Jakarta	1			
Jeddah			1	
Jerusalem			1	
Kampala			1	
Karachi			1	
Kathmandu				1
Kiev			1	
Kingston			1	
Kinshasa			1	
Kolonia			1	
Koror			1	
Kuala Lumpur			1	
Kuwait			1	
La Paz			1	
Lagos			1	
Lahore			1	
Lilongwe			1	
Lima			1	
Lisbon			1	
Ljubljana			1	
Lome			1	
London		1		
Luanda			1	

TABLE 4-1 Continued

Post	Science Counselor[a]	Science Officer	Part-Time Officer	Environmental Hub
Lusaka			1	
Madrid		1		
Majuro			1	
Managua			1	
Manila			1	
Marseille			1	
Maputo			1	
Mbabane			1	
Melbourne			1	
Merida			1	
Mexico City	1	3		
Monrovia			1	
Monterrey			1	
Montevideo			1	
Montreal			1	
Moscow	1	4		
Mumbai			1	
Muscat			1	
Nagoya			1	
Naha			1	
Nairobi			1	
Naples			1	
Nassau			1	
N'djamena			1	
New Delhi			1	
Niamey			1	
Nicosia			1	
Nouakchott			1	
Osaka Kobe			1	
Oslo			1	
Ottawa	1	1		
Ouagadougou			1	
Panama			1	
Paris	1	2		
Paris – OECD	1			
Perth			1	
Peshawar			1	
Phnom Penh			1	
Ponta Delgada			1	
Port-of-Spain			1	
Port Moresby			1	
Prague		1		
Pretoria		1		1
Pusan			1	
Quito			1	
Rabat			1	

TABLE 4-1 Continued

Post	Science Counselor[a]	Science Officer	Part-Time Officer	Environmental Hub
Rangoon			1	
Reykjavik			1	
Rio de Janeiro			1	
Riyadh			1	
Rome		1		
San Jose				1
San Salvador			1	
Sanaa			1	
Santiago			1	
Santo Domingo			1	
Sapporo			1	
Sarajevo			1	
Seoul	1		1	
Shanghai			1	
Shenyang			1	
Singapore			1	
Sofia			1	
St. Petersburg			1	
Stockholm			1	
Surabaya			1	
Suva			1	
Sydney			1	
Tashkent				1
Tegucigalpa			1	
Tel Aviv		1		
The Hague			1	
Thessaloniki			1	
Tokyo	1	4		1
Toronto			1	
Tunis		1		
Ulaanbaatar			1	
UNVIE Vienna	1	2		
UN New York			2	
Valletta			1	
Vancouver			1	
Vienna			1	
Vientiane			1	
Vladivostok			1	
Warsaw			1	
Wellington			1	
Yaounde			1	
Zagreb			1	

[a]Science Counselor category includes three people with the title "Minister-Counselor."
SOURCE: Department of State, OES, July 14, 1999.

U.S. diplomats involved in STH activities is impressive. However, the absence of Science Counselors at many important posts is surprising, and the weak technical credentials of most of the incumbent Science Counselors is striking and indeed alarming to many members of the U.S. STH communities. There is a sharp contrast between the Department's approach and the approach of most industrialized countries (e.g., France, Sweden) and indeed many developing nations (e.g., Mexico, Korea), which staff key embassies with technically trained specialists.

The current incumbents of the 10 Science Counselor positions are all FSOs, and most of the other Science Officer positions are filled with FSOs. Some have experience within the Department or at other posts in handling issues with substantial STH content. Most have had short courses in some aspect of STH at FSI. OES participates in the screening of candidates for these positions and often seeks candidates with STH experience. Overall, however, the level of STH competence of personnel assigned to U.S. embassies and the quality of their reporting on activities of interest to the U.S. STH communities have declined significantly in recent years, according to reports from Department officials, officials of other departments and agencies, and independent experts. These reports are consistent with personal observations of committee members.

At a few embassies, members of the country teams, other than Department personnel, have significant backgrounds in STH. In Tokyo and Paris, for example, the National Science Foundation (NSF) and other agencies have specialists on site. In Moscow there are sizable staffs of the National Aeronautics and Space Administration (NASA) and the Department of Energy (DOE) associated with the Embassy. In almost all embassies there are defense attachés, including many with formal training in STH disciplines. In a number of embassies there are specialists from the Department of Agriculture, the Department of Commerce, and the Agency for International Development (USAID) with in-depth knowledge of certain types of STH-related activities being carried out in the country. Also, in many embassies there are FSNs with technical training and/or considerable experience in following STH developments in the host countries.

At times, the foregoing talent may be overlooked when individual embassy officers address STH issues. Indeed, the Ambassador and the Deputy Chief of Mission may be unaware of the entire array of technical talent available to the embassies, although this is less likely at posts where a Science Counselor has a broad portfolio of responsibilities that subsumes activities managed by specialists from a variety of agencies. A full inventory of STH talent available at a post can be a valuable asset for the conduct of the business of the embassy. Also, the Department should reach agreement with other departments and agencies on how their personnel can most effectively assist the embassies and missions when called upon.

In every region of the world there are resident U.S. technical experts who may not be affiliated with the embassies but who are willing to provide information and advice to them if called upon. An excellent example is the Office of Naval Research contingents in London and Tokyo, staffed with highly qualified specialists in several technical fields. Multinational companies and American universities have many employees living abroad who are expert in some aspects of STH, and this resident cadre of specialists is frequently supplemented with short-term visitors.

In addition to this significant resource of specialists who are nearby, the Internet and other telecommunications channels have dramatically increased the amount of information available to the embassies, although there is a major problem in filtering authoritative information from less reliable reports. At the same time, departments and agencies in Washington, D.C., and U.S. private-sector institutions have greatly increased their direct communications with counterparts abroad, with significant implications for the role of Science Officers in collecting information that is not redundant but of genuine interest in Washington.

FRAMEWORK FOR STAFFING STH NEEDS IN U.S. EMBASSIES

Against the backdrop of existing staffing patterns and the decline in the number of Science Counselors with strong technical backgrounds, the importance of having skilled personnel assessing emerging issues, promoting activities of other departments and agencies, and interacting with senior host country STH officials has increased and will continue to grow. Indeed, as indicated in current staffing patterns, there is a need for some level of STH competence at almost every post.

In assessing the need for Science Counselors and the levels of STH competence required, the specific roles that the Science Counselors can be expected to fill are important. (See Appendix H for a standard position description of a Science Counselor or Science Officer.) The assessment will vary with the importance of the country, the significance of STH-related issues in U.S. foreign policy, budgetary pressure for competing positions, and the changing interests of ambassadors and other senior embassy personnel. Table 4-2 provides an approach to assessing staffing needs.

Given the wide variety of STH developments of interest throughout the world, the approach to overseas staffing should parallel the approach to filling the STH-related personnel needs of the Department in Washington. The Department should draw on a flexible mix of talent in various personnel categories, including STH specialists from industry or

TABLE 4-2   Embassy and Mission STH Staffing—An Illustrative Framework

Type of Post or Mission	STH Experience or Skills Required
Posts with broad and important STH interests (London, Paris, Moscow, Beijing, Tokyo, and others)	A highly trained Science Counselor; one or more R&D agency detailees; one or more FSOs; several FSNs (mix depends on issues)
Posts where a single issue dominates the STH-related agenda (IAEA)	A Science Counselor specialized in the issue; one or more R&D agency detailees
Posts in large and important developing countries (New Delhi, Mexico City, others)	A Science Counselor, highly trained or with strong STH-related experience in development assistance; one or more FSOs; several FSNs (mix depends on issues)
Missions to regional organizations with STH functions (OECD, EU, NATO, OAS)	A Science Counselor with broad technical background; one or more R&D agency detailees; one or more FSOs
Posts with part-time STH needs	One FSO with STH training; FSNs
Hubs with regional environmental responsibilities	One FSO with environmental training; one or more FSNs posted in the countries served
Hubs providing regional STH support for several embassies[a]	A Science Counselor; one or more FSNs posted in the countries served

NOTE: IAEA = International Atomic Energy Agency; EU = European Union; NATO = North Atlantic Treaty Organization; OECD = Organization for Economic Cooperation and Development; OAS = Organization of American States.

[a]This type of post does not now exist; it is suggested as a way of providing STH expertise for a cluster of posts in a geographic region.

academia, FSOs, career civil servants from the Department, and personnel borrowed from other departments and agencies. In some cases, a specialist who is already assigned overseas to represent the interests of another department or agency might serve in a "dual-hatted" capacity as a science officer.

Against this background, the case is strong for assigning highly trained specialists in STH to the position of Science Counselor at a number of important posts where STH-related issues of considerable foreign policy interest are on the agenda. Department officials currently responsible for staffing these positions argue that Science Counselors engage primarily in diplomacy and not the details of STH development, deal in very general terms with a wide range of technical issues well beyond the expertise of any single individual, and therefore do not need credentials in a specific technical discipline. The conclusion is weak, particularly given the importance of the Science Counselors' constant interactions with both U.S. and local specialists who have strong technical credentials. Although no individual can speak with authority on all technical subjects that cross his or her desk, in-depth competence in one aspect of STH significantly enhances personal capabilities to understand the key elements of other complex issues. Also, a record of personal STH achievements facilitates access to and improves rapport with high-level officials of the host government who are dealing with STH issues. The committee reviewed a number of examples of how technically trained Science Counselors were able to establish personal credibility with foreign colleagues, which resulted in continuing access to important organizations and specialists beyond what would normally be available to FSOs.

In rare cases, the type of STH experience and credibility that are needed might be found within the Foreign Service, and selected FSOs should be encouraged to develop the skills necessary for these assignments. In practice, however, most qualified candidates for Science Counselor posts should be brought in from outside the Department on limited-term appointments to avoid ambiguity as to their status within the Foreign Service. Of course, they must be carefully selected to ensure that, in addition to having STH credentials, they have experience and are effective in operating in a foreign policy environment. The excellent candidates attracted by the AAAS Fellows program show that there is a strong pool of interested individuals with the necessary technical backgrounds as well as foreign policy awareness.

Thus, at the core of the Department's overseas STH capabilities should be a cadre of highly qualified Science Counselors assigned to important embassies and missions in accordance with the following recommendation:[4]

Recommendation: *The Department should assign at least 25 carefully selected Science Counselors to embassies in countries where STH-related activities are of major interest to the U.S. Government*

---

[4]Candidate countries and missions are the United Kingdom, France, Germany, Russia, China, Republic of Korea, Japan, Mexico, Brazil, Chile, India, Israel, Middle East Regional (Cairo), West Africa Regional (Lagos), Southeast Asia Regional (Bangkok), Scandinavia Regional (Stockholm), European Union, North Atlantic Treaty Organization, Organization for Economic Cooperation and Development, Organization of American States, International Atomic Energy Agency, World Health Organization, World Meteorological Organization, United Nations Food and Agriculture Organization, and United Nations Headquarters.

and to missions to international and regional organizations that support STH programs of considerable foreign policy significance.

Most of these Science Counselors would fill positions that are already designated as Science Counselor or Science Officer positions. Since, however, some Science Officer positions would be upgraded to a more senior level, there would be increased costs. One proposal that should be explored is whether other departments or agencies (e.g., NSF, the National Institutes of Health [NIH], NASA, the National Oceanic and Atmospheric Administration [NOAA], the National Institute of Standards and Technology, DOE) might be willing to share some of these increased costs.

At the same time, FSOs serving in a variety of capacities other than Science Counselors or Science Officers will continue to handle many STH issues within the embassies. Political officers negotiate agreements concerning access to research facilities and technical information and participate in the development of positions on nuclear, space, and other high-visibility issues. Economic officers are concerned with the protection of intellectual property and the activities of high-technology multinational companies. Visa officers must be aware of local health conditions as well as the demand for high-technology skills in the United States. Administrative officers are responsible for ensuring adequate and clean drinking water, security barriers, and modern telecommunications within embassies and other diplomatic outposts. In short, from the Ambassador down to the lower ranks, the need for STH literacy in many types of assignments is increasing, thus reinforcing the earlier recommendation that all FSOs and other Department officials should have a basic level of STH literacy and awareness of the relevance of STH developments to foreign policy concerns.

Meanwhile, the Department has begun to emphasize regional responsibilities of environmental officers stationed at embassy hubs. This concept of regional coverage might also be applied to other areas of STH, with STH hubs providing support for activities at nearby smaller embassies. Such support might include, for example, representation and reporting visits by STH specialists from the embassy hubs to selected ministries in the other countries in response to requests from the posts or the Department. Aside from the environmental hubs, at present there are no examples of regional STH responsibilities based in the embassies, although in the past some Science Counselors had regional responsibilities. Opportunities frequently arise for upgrading STH literacy at senior levels during consultations in Washington of U.S. ambassadors who are assigned abroad. OES, PM, and EB need to take greater initiative to arrange consultations for ambassadors with the departments and agencies that support significant STH activities in the countries where they are accredited. The operation of a satellite tracking station, a visit by an oceano-graphic ship, an investigation of an unknown virus, and an exchange of medical isotopes are examples of STH programs that can be of high political visibility and can provide the ambassadors with important political assets.

Also, FSOs scheduled to assume duties as Science Officers, including environmental hub officers, can benefit greatly from specially designed STH training programs of at least four weeks' duration prior to assuming overseas duties. FSI has experience with this type of training, which emphasizes a customized set of consultations with government agencies that support programs in the countries of assignments.

SUPPORTING FIELD OPERATIONS

Reporting from the Field

The regional bureaus regularly provide embassies with guidance on their reporting interests. This guidance sometimes includes topics that have considerable STH content, although the topics may be categorized as security, trade, or economic issues. Occasionally, other offices of the Department issue guidelines on their program plans, which also assist the embassies in setting priorities for their activities. Appendix I, for example, highlights the goals and objectives set forth by OES as of August 1999. As can be seen, OES focuses to a significant degree on environmental and ocean issues but at the same time seems to neglect other important STH topics that have been identified in this report and that should be on the agenda of both OES and the embassies. Embassies and missions should be aware of issues of interest to other departments and agencies. The STH Senior Advisor should assist in ensuring that the Department develops reporting requirements that cover a broader range of interagency interests than is reflected in Appendix I. The involvement of the departments and agencies in articulating reporting requirements is important not only to highlight information of interest to them but also to avoid requesting information from embassies and missions that the departments and agencies can more easily obtain through their direct contacts with counterpart organizations abroad.

Many embassies now have web sites where they post information about recent developments in the country of interest. In some cases, the Science Officers have their own home pages. A particularly impressive home page is maintained by the Environment, Science, and Technology Section of the Embassy in Beijing (http://www.usembassy-china.gov/english/sandt/index.html), which has received favorable comments from a number of users in the United States.

FSI has initiated an important program to acquaint FSNs working in the STH area with developments in Washington and to arrange for them to meet with key personnel in other departments and agencies. FSNs shoulder much of the routine STH loads at the embassies, particularly in preparing unclassified reports for wide dissemination, and they have become indispensable fixtures at many posts. Thus, FSI efforts to familiarize them with their constituencies in Washington should be expanded.

In terms of requests from the embassies for STH-related information, the Department's emphasis should be on linking the embassies directly with information sources, which are often outside the Department. Once modern communications links are in place between the embassies and information sources, there is usually not a need for the Department offices to be in the middle of requests for technical information.

Integration of State and USAID Field Capabilities

USAID has had stronger field capabilities than the embassies in some areas such as agriculture, population, environment, and health. Frequently, although not always, embassy officers have been able to rely on USAID to provide information and expert assessment in these areas. As USAID downsizes, however, it is fast losing many competent scientific personnel, with a degradation of its STH presence in many countries. This in turn reduces its capability to support the Department's efforts overseas. A joint State/USAID study of the direct and indirect foreign policy, as well as the programmatic, impacts of USAID's reduction of technical staff would be useful in assessing the Department's needs for additional STH capabilities abroad. At the same time, USAID is becoming increasingly integrated into the Department, and greater attention should be given to the utilization of USAID's staff capability as a part of an enhanced STH foreign policy workforce.

Also of concern, the Department has established environmental hubs in some areas of the world where USAID has long had environmental programs. Although the role of the hubs is to report on developments and to consult with host governments on global environmental issues, some hubs would be greatly strengthened if they also took advantage of USAID's programmatic base, particularly long-standing agriculture and health expertise. In some regions the financial dimensions of environmental issues of interest to USAID are sufficiently important to open many doors to discuss policy issues.

Embassy Interactions with U.S. Government Visitors

In many countries, hundreds of U.S. government travelers visit counterparts every month. Although these visitors occasionally may burden embassy staffs with their administrative and logistical assistance requests, they nevertheless constitute an invaluable resource for the embassies since they usually have excellent access to important STH leaders and bring with them a wealth of knowledge about important international programs and related STH developments around the world. Some government visitors regularly consult with the embassies, whereas others are unaware of the ways in which the embassies could be helpful to them or they to the embassies.

Moreover, a number of agency specialists have successfully served as Science Counselors and as representatives of their departments and agencies abroad. Thus, they are quite familiar with the needs of the embassies and can be helpful to the embassies in staying abreast of the interests in Washington.

5

Interagency Interests and Opportunities

OVERLOADING THE CAPABILITIES OF THE DEPARTMENT

STH considerations dominate many of the interactions between the Department and other departments and agencies. As a result of the soaring volume and increasing complexity of these interactions, *traditional mechanisms for handling the Department's relations with other departments and agencies are overloaded.* There are growing concerns that at times (1) foreign policy decisions may not give adequate weight to the views of important elements of the governmental STH community and (2) interagency reviews and coordination may unnecessarily delay or complicate the implementation of international programs of the departments and agencies.

According to one analysis, more than 60 departments and agencies support international STH activities carried out through more than 200 programs, with many programs consisting of large numbers of projects; the annual expenditures for these programs exceed $1 billion.[1] Against this broad panorama of activities, the committee reviewed the interests and selected activities of eight departments and agencies; they are responsible for about 90 percent of the federal civilian R&D budget and

---

[1]Interagency Working Group on U.S. Government-Sponsored International Exchanges and Training, *1997 Annual Report*, p. 6. Available from the Office of Exchange Coordination, Bureau of Educational and Cultural Affairs, U.S. Information Agency, Washington, DC 20547-0001 (telephone 202-260-5124).

therefore represent much of the STH capabilities supported by the U.S. Government. The committee gave particular emphasis to long-duration international commitments, programs, and projects while recognizing that often *ad hoc* projects of short duration can also be important both to the STH community and to the Department. Although each department and agency has its own particular set of international interests, some common threads warrant attention.

The international interests and programs of most departments and agencies are expanding. A large number of activities are mandated in legislation (International Space Station [NASA], protection of nuclear material in Russia [DOE]). Of these, many are extensions of domestic programs that are affected by international developments or can benefit from international cooperation (environmental protection of the Great Lakes [Environmental Protection Agency, EPA], oceanographic investigations in foreign waters [NOAA]). Other programs flow from the policies and priorities of intergovernmental and other international organizations (World Health Organization [WHO] programs on infectious diseases [Department of Health and Human Services, HHS]). Still others are undertaken to obtain scientific inputs from foreign researchers or to share costs with interested foreign organizations.

A few international STH activities receive continuing attention at the highest levels of the executive and legislative branches in Washington (e.g., global climate change, nuclear nonproliferation regime, U.S.-Japan cooperation and reciprocal access to Japanese technological developments). The impacts of specific incidents involving U.S. researchers on bilateral scientific relations can sometimes be profound, as reflected in recent reports concerning the mishandling of nuclear weapons data at U.S. laboratories. At the other extreme, many cooperative activities of individual researchers supported with government funds attract very little attention, including projects that may have global or regional implications (e.g., research grants for individual investigators awarded by NIH and NSF).

In short, the departments and agencies are widening their global perspectives and expanding their international activities. International organizations are finding greater political support for a variety of global programs involving STH issues that are central to the missions of the departments and agencies. American industry and American scientific organizations are increasingly looking for support from the departments and agencies as they strengthen their international activities. Thus, the responsibilities of the Department for staying abreast of and assisting with these types of activities will continue to grow. To carry out these responsibilities, the Department must have effective mechanisms for interacting with many elements of the U.S. Government.

TYPES OF INTERAGENCY INTERACTIONS

Many types of interagency interactions have been in place for decades. New interactions usually are linked to initiatives of individual departments and agencies. Sometimes initiatives originate in the White House. Often foreign governments propose new programs, and their proposals require responses that sometimes involve cooperative activities. On occasion, the Department stimulates STH programs of other departments and agencies in order to serve foreign policy objectives. Whatever the origin of an international activity, the Department seeks to ensure that it is consistent with foreign policy objectives while the originator of the proposal seeks a foreign policy that will facilitate, or at least accommodate, the activity.

Among the most important types of interagency interactions in addressing international STH activities are the following:

• *Coordinated support of five vice-presidential-level bilateral commissions,* which accord considerable priority to cooperation in STH (i.e., commissions involving Russia, China, Ukraine, South Africa, Egypt).

• *Development of the concepts, frameworks, and details of umbrella intergovernmental STH agreements,* which are coordinated and negotiated by the Department and counterpart ministries of foreign affairs: The activities carried out within the framework of these umbrella agreements are usually the responsibility of selected departments and agencies. Thirty-three umbrella agreements are in place with a new agreement with Vietnam currently being developed.

• *Review and approval of requests from the agencies for authorization for negotiating and signing memoranda of understanding (MOUs):* More than 790 MOUs with STH content are in place, not including those in the national security area. The Department considers 90 percent to be "binding" and therefore requiring action on the part of the U.S. Government.[2] Many MOUs are within the framework of umbrella agreements, while others

---

[2]This estimate was provided in March 1999 by a Department official charged with tracking such agreements. A definitive total is unavailable due to the discontinuation of reporting requirements that previously existed under Title V. The effort required to prepare the reports was deemed to far outweigh their value. However, there is now a need for more accurate accounting of international STH agreements. In addition, the 790 figure does not include the large number of contracts and other subagreements to implement programs. For example, NASA has 3,000 active international "agreements" of some type. A discussion of the international agreements of a number of key departments and agencies is included in "Federal Research: Information on International Science and Technology Agreements," United States General Accounting Office, April 1999, GAO/RCED-99-108.

are independent of umbrella agreements. The process of gaining approvals to negotiate and/or sign MOUs (as well as umbrella agreements), referred to as the Circular 175 process, involves the concurrence of interested Department offices, particularly the Office of Legal Adviser, and other agencies that have an interest, such as the Office of the Trade Representative, which is particularly concerned with intellectual property rights.

• *Support of bilateral STH relationships not called for in formal agreements:* Most countries want to have some type of STH relationship with the United States with or without agreements, and most of the time such arrangements involve departments or agencies using either their own budgetary resources or funds provided through USAID. In any event, U.S. embassies are under constant pressure from local STH communities to expand bilateral cooperation, and requests for locating interested partners for cooperative projects frequently end up on the desks of the departments and agencies.

• *Assistance in gaining access to facilities, people, and geographic areas:* Some programs require special arrangements for access to territorial waters, airspace, sensitive government facilities, environmental samples, and biological specimens. These arrangements usually involve formal requests from the Department to counterpart governments. As one example, in 1998 the Department requested clearances for more than 300 voyages by U.S. research vessels, with each voyage involving, on average, access to the territorial waters of more than three countries. Thus, the Department, acting through the embassies, sent about 1,000 diplomatic notes requesting clearance, received 1,000 answers, and took steps to ensure that trip reports were filed with each of the governments granting access. In some countries local scientists joined the cruises, and additional diplomatic interactions were necessary.[3]

• *Support of activities of international organizations and multilateral negotiations:* With more than two dozen major international organizations having significant interests in STH developments, the Department requires (1) preparation of a continuing stream of position papers touching on many interagency issues; (2) designation of members of delegations from a variety of departments and agencies to meetings of the organizations; (3) implementation of internationally agreed-upon programs that draw on the resources of the departments and agencies; and (4) budget negotiations in Washington to obtain the required and voluntary contributions to the organizations.

---

[3]This estimate was provided in March 1999 by a Department official responsible for tracking these clearances.

- *U.S. responses to major security and humanitarian crises* (e.g., resettlement activities in Kosovo, continuing confrontations in Iraq, devastation from Hurricane Mitch, demining challenges in Bosnia, refugee problems in Rwanda, forest fires in Southeast Asia): STH capabilities of the departments and agencies support such responses in many ways in addition to military responses, including the deployment of high-technology communications equipment, provision of medical and food support, advice on approaches for stopping degradation of agricultural lands and water supplies, and predictions of impending droughts and floods.

- *Removal of impediments encountered in implementing long-duration international programs:* Even though programs may have been operating overseas successfully for many years, there are often administrative or policy issues that arise and can be resolved only through intervention by the Department with the counterpart foreign ministry.

- *Facilitation of programs in the United States involving foreign participation:* Foreign participants usually require visas, and on occasion there may be foreign policy or security objections to their proposed activities in the United States (e.g., access to DOE weapons laboratories, Cuban visitors).

- *Individual consultations and visits by agency officials, scientists, and contractor personnel abroad:* These consultations may be to review activities underway, to coordinate shared program interests, or to explore the possibility of initiating new activities. In some cases, significant foreign policy issues may be involved, although in many cases there should be little need for the Department to follow the technical issues.

- *Acquisition and dissemination of information concerning STH developments abroad:* Although various departments and agencies have direct connections with counterpart agencies and individuals abroad and can obtain a great deal of information through their own networks, the embassies are often in a position to provide the broad science policy context within which technical activities are being carried out. Also, the embassies may be the first to learn of high-level personnel shifts or budgetary decisions that are significant to the departments and agencies.

- *Coordination of overlapping interagency interests and resolution of interagency disagreements:* Many international programs are of interest to several departments and agencies with complementary capabilities. Also, there are often conflicts among the economic, security, and technical interests of the departments and agencies that need to be resolved. The Department frequently assumes responsibility for ensuring that interagency problems are addressed and, if necessary, sent to the Office of the President for resolution.

- *Use of the Department's external program funds:* The offices subordinate to the Undersecretary for Global Affairs and the Undersecretary for

Arms Control and International Security administer STH-related program funds totaling hundreds of millions of dollars annually (e.g., humanitarian assistance, counternarcotics activities, environmental diplomacy workshops, U.S.-Israeli bilateral foundations, science centers in Russia and Ukraine, nonproliferation programs). Frequently, other departments and agencies play critical roles in the implementation of programs supported by these funds, and the Department must ensure that the programs are responsive to a variety of interagency interests.

• *Support of U.S. industrial interests abroad:* There are frequently concerns over the activities of U.S. companies abroad, particularly in balancing the promotion of private-sector economic interests with export control limitations and with constraints imposed by U.S. economic sanctions. The views of the Department and other departments and agencies may diverge on such issues.

Obviously, these types of interagency interactions cover a broad spectrum of day-to-day activities, ranging from the issuance of individual visas to negotiation of global regimes that affect activities in many countries. The interests and involvement of the departments and agencies are manifold, and only through effective interagency partnerships can the Department assume an international leadership role in a broad range of STH-related activities or even meet its minimal international obligations.

IMPROVING INTERAGENCY PROCESSES

Transferring Responsibilities for Selected Activities

Although resource constraints are a central consideration in efforts of the Department to upgrade its capabilities to interact with other departments and agencies, significant steps to improve efficiency in interagency forums should be possible without large influxes of new resources. As discussed in Chapter 2, additional resources are clearly warranted in some areas, but realistically the Department will have many demands on new resources that become available, and support of interagency activities may not be its highest priority.

Thus, it is important to face directly the reality that the Department simply does not, and probably will not, have sufficient personnel or the technical wherewithal to adequately discharge all of its current STH-related responsibilities, let alone assume additional responsibilities as new opportunities for integrating STH capabilities with foreign policy objectives arise. At the same time, it appears that some activities currently managed by the Department could be managed effectively by other departments and agencies.

Recommendation: *The Department, in consultation with other departments and agencies, should transfer responsibilities for STH activities to other appropriate and willing departments and agencies whenever there is not a compelling reason for retaining responsibilities within the Department.*

Of course, the departments and agencies should keep the Department informed of developments where significant or sensitive foreign policy issues are involved. Indeed, the deliberate transfer of responsibilities with continuing coordination should be more effective in ensuring an integration of STH activities and foreign policy than a situation whereby other departments and agencies undertake international activities on their own and simply avoid the Department due to the overload in its administrative and foreign policy channels.

By dispersing selected responsibilities to departments and agencies capable of adequately handling them, the Department should be able to move toward a better balance of responsibilities and available resources. For example, consideration should be given to having NSF play an expanded role in managing the activities of the bilateral U.S.-Israeli foundations. NOAA might take on the task of preparing the paperwork for all requests for research ship clearances, with State being responsible only for the negotiation of requests with counterpart foreign ministries. In terms of emerging issues, NSF might be given responsibility for addressing the scientific dimensions of intellectual property rights that are of concern internationally, whereas HHS, working with USAID, might be assigned the lead for formulating international policies to address the suppression of infectious diseases.

This list is just a beginning, and a systematic review of opportunities for transfers of responsibilities is in order. Of course the departments and agencies that are asked to assume greater responsibilities may want to obtain additional personnel and financial resources; and the resource issue must be addressed prior to transferring responsibilities. In some cases, consolidating responsibilities within other departments or agencies already devoting resources to the activities of interest should reduce the total resource requirements for managing the programs, although resource requirements will have to be analyzed on a case-by-case basis.

There are many examples of departments and agencies other than the Department having the primary role for programs and negotiations of international organizations (e.g., USAID at the OECD Development Assistance Committee, HHS at WHO, NOAA at the World Meteorological Organization, EPA at the OECD Chemicals Committee). Expansion of this practice could help reduce the problem of overload. For example, there seems to be no reason for EPA not to assume more responsibility for

U.S. participation in the United Nations Environment Programme and in the negotiation of a new toxic substances agreement. Consideration should be given to having NSF serve as the agency responsible for liaison with the United Nations Educational, Scientific, and Cultural Organization in the absence of U.S. membership in this organization. NSF and the Department of Commerce might take on greater responsibility for science and technology activities at OECD. All of these shifts should open opportunities for the staffs of the other departments and agencies to take on much of the preparatory burden for meetings that is currently shouldered by Department officials.

The Circular 175 Process

The Circular 175 process calls for review by appropriate offices of the Department and by other interested departments and agencies, as determined by the Department, of each proposal for a new or modified international agreement. Most of these proposals originate within individual departments and agencies. This is a major activity, with dozens of proposed STH agreements under review at any given time. The process is filled with inefficiencies and delays, and administrative problems associated with the process are at the root of many interagency conflicts. Also, foreign collaborators eager to enter into cooperative activities are often bewildered and apprehensive concerning bureaucratic delays in establishing the necessary political framework for cooperation.

Recommendation: *The Department, in consultation with the Office of Management and Budget (OMB) and other departments and agencies, should streamline the Circular 175 process, which calls for interagency reviews of proposed international agreements and bilateral memoranda of understanding.*

Many international activities are carried out without the need for an MOU or other formal agreement that is subject to the Circular 175 process. Clearer guidelines are needed as to when a proposed activity reaches the threshold of a formal agreement and therefore needs Circular 175 clearance and when and how a dormant agreement should be canceled, keeping in mind the interests of other governments that may have budgetary or other reasons for requiring and maintaining formal agreements. To ease the process of canceling meaningless agreements, the "sunset" provisions now included in some agreements might become a regular component of agreements unless there are compelling reasons against such provisions.

Several steps should ease the Circular 175 clearance process. First, the Department should prepare standard language for commonly used provisions of agreements in addition to the language already available for intellectual property rights, business confidential information, and national security interests. Second, the Department should encourage the adoption of language in MOUs that conforms to the language of umbrella agreements when such overarching agreements are in place. Third, each agency should consider developing or adopting user-friendly handbooks for its staff on how to prepare an MOU similar to the handbook of the Department of Energy.

Role of the Department in Implementing STH Agreements

The details of many international projects are reviewed in interagency forums many times over—as they are developed, modified, and implemented. The initial reviews are important to ensure that proposed activities are consistent with foreign policy objectives, both on a global basis and in country-specific situations. In politically sensitive cases, the Department should monitor activities on a continuing basis, but most activities do not warrant intensive scrutiny by the Department.

Joint reviews by the Department and the concerned agencies each year or every two years of major, long-duration STH programs and projects could lead to interagency agreement on a reduced role for the Department during implementation activities once adequate coordination mechanisms are in place. Blanket clearances by the Department for activities abroad, including international travel, for specific projects whenever possible would seem appropriate. The administrative load of clearing travelers of other departments and agencies is staggering, with more than 50,000 STH-related travel clearances granted in 1998.[4]

Although considerable effort will be required to examine a number of the activities of several dozen departments and agencies, in the long run there should be considerable savings of staff time both within the Department and within other departments and agencies. In a few cases, the Department has given blanket travel authorizations for projects, but this is the rare exception. To ensure that the Department can monitor developments when blanket travel authorizations are granted, other departments and agencies should be required to inform the Department and the relevant embassies of impending international travel with sufficient lead time so the Department and embassies can disapprove the travel if there are overriding foreign policy considerations or administrative problems that dictate against it.

---

[4]This estimate was provided in July 1999 by Department officials responsible for handling a significant portion of the clearances.

Relations with the Office of Science and Technology Policy (OSTP)

For more than four decades, OSTP and its predecessor organizations have assembled advisory committees and led a number of interagency efforts concerning the role of STH in U.S. foreign policy. During the past several years, senior OSTP officials have had difficulty engaging senior Department officials in discussions concerning interagency coordination of STH activities. The key Department officials were fully occupied with other commitments.

OSTP can be a strong ally in broad foreign policy deliberations involving STH-related issues in which it may be a major player. Its role can be especially important when disagreements arise among departments and agencies or within the White House complex. In addition, it has both the technical skills and the organizational clout to help ensure that interagency interactions are meaningful. On a number of occasions in the past, OSTP has used its good offices to take over some of the interagency coordination burdens that would have otherwise fallen on the Department. Thus, the Department should give higher priority to working closely with OSTP. Finally, the Department should encourage OSTP, in cooperation with the National Security Council and the National Economic Council, to give greater attention to the nexus between domestic and international STH concerns so as to strengthen the requests of State and other departments and agencies for funding for international programs.

Rotation of Personnel from the Departments and Agencies

During the past several years, there have been impressive examples of detailees to the Department from other departments and agencies making important contributions to STH-related activities in Washington (e.g., PM, Office of the Legal Adviser, OES, EB) and abroad (e.g., embassies in Bonn and New Delhi). In some cases, the sending organizations have been sufficiently interested in strengthening the Department's technical capabilities to pay the costs of the detailee assignments. Sometimes, the detailees do not count against personnel ceilings of the Department. They can be quite helpful in reducing overload problems.

Although many offices of the Department effectively use detailees, few departments and agencies have a regularized program for providing detailees. The Department of Defense (DOD) is an important exception, and some offices of the Department can count on military officers being available to augment their staffs on a regular basis. Other offices use detailees whenever they can make the necessary arrangements, but they often miss opportunities to strengthen their technical capabilities because of the uncertainties associated with the availability of detailees.

Recommendation: *The Department should increase its use of specialists from other departments and agencies as rotating employees assigned to positions in Washington and abroad, as participants in international negotiations, and as advisors on topics in their areas of expertise.*

The Department's leadership should have a continuing dialogue with senior officials of the other departments and agencies on the mutual benefits from such involvement of technical personnel in its activities and should establish more effective mechanisms that will help ensure continued interagency support for addressing both ad hoc and recurring issues.

Budget Support

Although each technical agency must justify its own request for personnel and budget resources to support international activities, a united front before OMB and Congress can often be helpful in demonstrating synergism among programs and fending off criticisms of lack of coordination. Department leadership is sometimes appropriate in organizing interagency reviews involving OSTP and OMB, as well as other departments and agencies, regarding government-wide resource needs for developing and conducting high-priority STH-related international policies and programs. Also, at carefully selected opportunities, the Department should undertake joint efforts with other departments and agencies to request and justify needed funds on Capitol Hill.

SUSTAINED PARTNERSHIPS

Some of the nation's most successful foreign policy efforts have rested on close interagency working relationships. Successes at international fisheries negotiations have been attributable to effective collaboration between the Department and NOAA. A strong U.S. presence during negotiations on international allocation of radio frequencies rests on sustained interactions between the Department, the Federal Communications Commission, and several other agencies. U.S. leadership in establishing international security regimes has been the product of joint efforts of the Department, DOD, DOE, ACDA, and the intelligence community. The Department's success in mobilizing technical resources for combating international terrorism involves more than 40 departments and agencies.

In each of these efforts, a few key specialists from different departments and agencies have provided much of the glue that holds the interagency process together. Some have been on assignment to the Department, and FSOs have served in the cooperating departments and agencies. This interchange of personnel, together with the organizational adjustments recommended above, is ever more important as the foreign policy issues with STH content become more complex, deadlines become shorter, and stakes for the United States and the world become higher.

6

Epilogue

Revolutionary advances in communications networks, in biotechnology, and in sophisticated armaments exemplify how STH advances are transforming the international landscape. Electronic circuits transfer more than a trillion dollars across international borders every day. Improved pharmaceutical and agricultural products extend life expectancies on every continent. High-precision weapons have changed the meaning of warfare. The Department must be able to take full account of these and other achievements of American and foreign laboratories as it shapes America's foreign policy in the coming decades. At the same time, the world looks to the United States as the leader in many aspects of STH. Thus, the Department has the opportunity to capitalize on American STH achievements in assuming leadership in a multitude of areas of foreign policy that are driven by technological developments.

How can this be done? First and foremost, integration of the nation's STH expertise into the processes for developing and implementing foreign policy must be carried out on a sustained basis on many fronts. However, if the Department is to use the nation's assets effectively in achieving international political economic, security, and scientific objectives, it needs a workforce that is attuned to the STH content of foreign policy issues and motivated to use STH capabilities to their fullest. Although organizational adjustments and strengthened mechanisms for interfaces between the Department and the STH community are also important, such changes in and of themselves cannot substitute for action officers who know when and how to mobilize expertise in support of day-to-day policy-making and resolution of operational issues.

This report has emphasized the use of STH expertise in the formulation of foreign policy, or *science for diplomacy*. Of no less importance is the development of policies that will serve the interests of STH, or *diplomacy for science*. In reality, however, these two aspects of foreign policy are closely entwined. As the Department draws on STH expertise in developing policies, it identifies ways in which the STH community can launch programs in support of these policies, and as American specialists carry out international STH programs, they become prime sources of expertise as to how foreign policy can be configured to serve U.S. interests. For example, the contribution of STH exchanges as a stabilizing force in U.S. relations with the Soviet Union and as an opening wedge for relations with China brought together scientific and political objectives. The Green Revolution changed the economies and political orientation of many developing countries while advancing agricultural sciences on a broad front. STH cooperation is now an important part of the Middle East peace process, as both political leaders and scientists benefit from joint projects in the desert and along the coasts.

The recommendations set forth in this report take into account such major STH contributions to foreign policy in the past and provide a framework for even more impressive achievements in the future. They build on the current strengths of the Department, emphasizing that investments in developing additional STH competence throughout the Department will pay handsome rewards for U.S. foreign policy.

Appendixes

APPENDIX
A

Request for Study from the Department of State

United States Department of State

The Counselor

Washington, D.C. 20520

Dear Dr. Alberts:

Before he left the Department, Tim Wirth shared with Secretary Albright your candid and constructive discussions regarding the role of science, technology and health (ST&H) in U.S. foreign policy. As you know, the State Department takes its responsibilities in the area of ST&H very seriously. Science is critical to many areas of our foreign policy, as it contributes our international health, environmental quality, national security, economic success, and to meeting global needs for food, water, and energy. It also serves as the basis for many of our bilateral and international programs, such as the U.S.-Japan Common Agenda and scientist exchanges.

Nonetheless, we may not be doing as much in the science, technology and health areas as we can. As part of our ongoing efforts to ensure that these issues are reflected in our foreign policy in the best possible manner, the Secretary has asked me to request that the Academies collaborate with the State Department to study the contributions ST&H can make to foreign policy, and how the Department might better carry out its responsibilities to that end, within its resource constraints. I should note that the Office of Science and Technology Policy is aware of this request and supports this initiative.

The Academies have a long history of scientific excellence and international engagement, and is particularly suited to carry out such a study. I hope you will give this idea serious consideration.

Please contact Melinda Kimble, Acting Assistant Secretary of the Bureau of Oceans and International Environmental and Scientific Affairs, at (202) 647-1554 to discuss this idea further. We look forward to hearing from you.

Sincerely,

Wendy R. Sherman

Wendy R. Sherman

Dr. Bruce Alberts,
    President,
        National Academy of Sciences,
            2101 Constitution Ave., NW,
                Washington, DC 20418.

79

APPENDIX

B

Selected Studies on Science, Technology, and Foreign Affairs

Studies Sponsored by Department of State

Science and Foreign Relations, International Policy Survey Group, Department of State, 1950 (referred to as the "Berkner Report").

Glennan, T. Keith, *Technology and Foreign Affairs*, Department of State, 1976.

Science, Technology, and Foreign Affairs, four volumes, Foreign Service Institute, 1984.

Jones, Teresa C., *Science Attaches Now and Tomorrow*, Department of State, September 1, 1991.

Amenson, Pat, "Umbrella Science and Technology Agreements," Department of State, August 12, 1996 (draft report).

Environmental Diplomacy: The Environment and U.S. Foreign Policy, Department of State, April 1997.

Studies Sponsored by U.S. Congress

The Management of Global Issues, Commission on the Organization of Government for the Conduct of Foreign Policy, vol. 1, appendix B, U.S. Government Printing Office, June 1975.

Science and Technology in the Department of State: Bringing Technical Content into Diplomatic Policy and Operations, Subcommittee on International Security and Scientific Affairs, Committee on International Relations, U.S. House of Representatives, prepared by Congressional Research Service, 1975.

Science, Technology, and Diplomacy in the Age of Interdependence, Subcommittee on International Security and Scientific Affairs, Committee on International Relations, U.S. House of Representatives, prepared by Congressional Research Service, 1976.

Science, Technology, and American Diplomacy, Committee on International Relations, U.S. House of Representatives, three volumes, prepared by Congressional Research Service, 1977.

International Science, National Science Policy Study, Committee on Science, U.S. House of Representatives, report in preparation, 1998.

Studies of the National Academies

Scientific Communication and National Security, National Research Council, National Academy Press, 1983 (referred to as the "Corson Report").

Wallerstein, Mitchel B. (ed.), *Scientific and Technological Cooperation Among Industrialized Countries: The Role of the United States*, National Research Council, National Academy Press, 1984.

Keatley, Anne G. (ed.), *Technological Frontiers and Foreign Relations*, National Research Council, National Academy Press, 1985.

The Embassy of the Future: Recommendations for the Design of Future U.S. Embassy Buildings, National Research Council, 1986.

Balancing the National Interest: U.S. National Security, Export Controls, and Global Economic Cooperation, National Research Council, National Academy Press, 1987.

Strengthening U.S. Engineering Through International Cooperation: Some Recommendations for Action, National Academy of Engineering, National Academy Press, 1987.

Guile, B. R., and H. Brooks (eds.), *Technology and Global Industry: Companies and Nations in the World Economy*, National Academy of Engineering, National Academy Press, 1988.

Muroyama, J. H., and H. G. Stever (eds.), *Globalization of Technology: International Perspectives*, National Academy of Engineering, National Academy Press, 1988.

The Revolution in Information and Communications Technology and the Conduct of U.S. Foreign Affairs, National Research Council, National Academy Press, 1988.

Finding Common Ground: U.S. Export Controls in a Changed Global Environment, National Academy Press, 1991.

America's Vital Interest in Global Health, Institute of Medicine, National Academy Press, 1997.

The Future of U.S. Nuclear Weapons Policy, National Academy of Sciences, National Academy Press, 1997.

Maximizing U.S. Interests in Science and Technology Relations with Japan: Committee on Japan Framework Statement and Report of the Competitiveness Task Force, National Research Council, National Academy Press, 1997.

Proliferation Concerns: Assessing U.S. Efforts to Help Contain Nuclear and Other Dangerous Materials and Technologies in the Former Soviet Union, National Research Council, National Academy Press, 1997.

Global Economy, Global Technology, Global Corporations: Reports of a Joint Task Force of the National Research Council and the Japan Society for the Promotion of Science on the Rights and Responsibilities of Multinational Corporations in an Age of Technological Interdependence, National Research Council, National Academy Press, 1998.

Internet Counts: Measuring the Impacts of the Internet, National Research Council, National Academy Press, 1998.

Nelson, Joan M., Charles Tilley, and Lee Walker (eds.), *Transforming Post-Communist Political Economies*, National Research Council, National Academy Press, 1998.

Other Studies

Skolnikoff, Eugene B., *Science, Technology, and American Foreign Policy*, MIT Press, 1967.

Pollack, Herman, "Science and Technology Advice to the Secretary of State," George Washington University, 1988.

Science and Technology in U.S. International Affairs, Carnegie Commission on Science, Technology, and Government, January 1992.

International Environmental Research and Assessment: Proposals for Better Organization and Decision Making, Carnegie Commission on Science, Technology, and Government, July 1992.

Partnerships for Global Development: The Clearing Horizon, Carnegie Commission on Science, Technology, and Government, December 1992.

Science, Technology, and Government for a Changing World, Carnegie Commission on Science, Technology, and Government, April 1993.

Skolnikoff, Eugene B., *The Elusive Transformation: Science, Technology, and the Evolution of International Politics*, Princeton University Press, 1993.

APPENDIX
C

Biographies of Committee Members

**COMMITTEE ON THE SCIENCE, TECHNOLOGY, AND
HEALTH ASPECTS OF THE FOREIGN POLICY AGENDA
OF THE UNITED STATES**

Robert A. Frosch (*Chair*) is a theoretical physicist by education (A.B., Columbia College, 1947, and Ph.D., Columbia University, 1952). He conducted research in ocean acoustics and was Director of Hudson Laboratories at Columbia University. He later served as Director for Nuclear Test Detection and Deputy Director of the Advanced Research Projects Agency (ARPA) in the Department of Defense; Assistant Secretary of the Navy for Research and Development (ASNR&D); Assistant Executive Director of the United Nations Environment Programme (UNEP); Associate Director for Applied Oceanography of the Woods Hole Oceanographic Institution (WHOI); Administrator of NASA; President of the American Association of Engineering Societies (AAES); and Vice President of General Motors Corporation (GM) in charge of research laboratories. He retired from GM in 1993 before joining the John F. Kennedy School of Government of Harvard University, where he is an associate in the Robert and Renee Belfer Center for Science and International Affairs. He is a member of the National Academy of Engineering and the American Academy of Arts and Sciences, a foreign member of the UK Royal Academy of Engineering, and a fellow or member of a number of professional societies.

John D. Axtell is Lynn Distinguished Professor of Agronomy at Purdue University. He received his B.S. (1957) and M.S. (1965) from the University of Minnesota and Ph.D. (1967) in the area of genetics from the University of Wisconsin. He has had a distinguished career as a plant geneticist and educator and is considered a global leader in sorghum nutritional quality research, particularly in protein quality and digestibility. He pioneered and led the discovery of naturally occurring high-lysine mutants of sorghum in a systematic survey of the world sorghum collection. He later produced high-lysine mutations through chemical mutagenesis and carried out an extensive breeding program to transfer the high-lysine gene in an array of genetic backgrounds. He is a member of the National Academy of Sciences (1982) and has served as Chairman of Class VI (1994-1997) and Section 62 (1987-1990) of the Academy. He is a member of the McKnight Foundation Collaborative Crop Research Program (1993-1999) and of the Raymond and Mary Baker Council for Excellence in Agronomy at Iowa State University. He has served on several review missions both for national research programs in various developing countries and a number of international research centers.

Harry Barnes is Director of the Conflict Resolution Program of the Carter Center and Chair of the Center's Human Rights Committee. He joined the Carter Center in 1994 as Director of its Conflict Resolution Program. He also oversees staff activities to promote human rights and prevent abuses and works closely with the center's International Human Rights Council. He was Ambassador to Romania from 1974 to 1977, Ambassador to India from 1981 to 1985, and Ambassador to Chile from 1985 to 1988 during the last years of the Pinochet regime. Among other assignments, he served as Director-General and Director of Personnel of the U.S. Foreign Service and as Deputy Executive Secretary for the Department of State. He began his 30-year career with the Foreign Service as an officer in Bombay, Prague, Moscow, Kathmandu, Bucharest, and Washington, D.C. He retired from the Department of State in 1988. He earned a bachelor's degree from Amherst College and a master's degree from Columbia University's Russian Institute.

Gail H. Cassell is Vice President of Infectious Diseases Research at Eli Lilly and Company, Lilly Research Laboratories, in Indianapolis. She was previously the Charles H. McCauley Professor and Chairman of the Department of Microbiology at the University of Alabama Schools of Medicine and Dentistry in Birmingham. A recent past president of the American Society for Microbiology, she just completed a three-year term as a member of the National Institutes of Health Director's Advisory Committee and as a member of the Advisory Council of the National Institute of

Allergy and Infectious Diseases of NIH. She was named to the original Board of Scientific Councilors of the Center for Infectious Diseases, Centers for Disease Control and Prevention, and later served as chair of this board. A member of the Institute of Medicine, she serves on several editorial boards of scientific journals and has authored more than 250 articles and book chapters. Beyond her scientific research work, she has been intimately involved in the establishment of science policy and legislation on biomedical research and public health, serving as Chairman of the Public and Scientific Affairs Board of the American Society for Microbiology and previously serving as an advisor on infectious diseases and indirect research costs to the White House Office of Science and Technology Policy.

Sue E. Eckert is Senior Fellow at the Thomas J. Watson Jr. Institute for International Studies at Brown University and Visiting Fellow at the Institute for International Economics in Washington, D.C. From 1993 to 1997, she was Assistant Secretary of Commerce for Export Administration, where she administered a range of U.S. export control and defense industrial base programs. Previously she served on the professional staff of the Committee on Foreign Affairs of the U.S. House of Representatives, specializing in technology transfer, international trade, and national security and nonproliferation export control issues. She has also worked extensively with business and nonprofit groups as an independent trade consultant, as well as lectured on foreign policy and national security decision-making issues.

Robert W. Fri is Director of the National Museum of Natural History of the Smithsonian Institution and Senior Fellow Emeritus at Resources for the Future, where he served as President from 1986 to 1995. He is a director of the American Electric Power Company and of Hagler Bailly, Inc., an international consulting firm specializing in natural resources and environmental issues. He is also a member of the University of Chicago Board of Governors for the Argonne National Laboratory and a trustee of Science Service, Inc., publisher of *Science News* and organizer of the Intel Science Talent Search. Earlier in his career he served as the Deputy Administrator of the U.S. Environmental Protection Agency and of the Energy Research and Development Administration.

David Hamburg is President Emeritus at Carnegie Corporation of New York, after having been President from 1983 to 1997. He received his A.B. (1944) and his M.D. (1947) degrees from Indiana University. He was Chief, Adult Psychiatry Branch, NIMH, from 1958 to 1961; Professor and Chairman of the Department of Psychiatry and Behavioral Sciences from 1961 to 1972; Reed-Hodgson Professor of Human Biology at Stanford University from 1972 to 1976; President of the Institute of Medicine, National Academy of Sciences, 1975-1980; Director of the Division of Health Policy Research and Education and John D. MacArthur Professor of Health Policy at Harvard University, 1980-1983. He served as President and then Chairman of the Board (1984-1986) of the American Association for the Advancement of Science. He was Chairman of the Carnegie Council on Adolescent Development (1986-1996). He is a member of the President's Committee of Advisors on Science and Technology, Visiting Professor at Harvard Medical School's Department of Social Medicine, and Co-chair (with Cyrus Vance) of the Carnegie Commission on Preventing Deadly Conflict. He received the American Psychiatric Association's Distinguished Service Award in 1991, the Presidential Medal of Freedom at the White House in September 1996, the International Peace Academy's 25th Anniversary Special Award in December 1996, the Achievement in Children and Public Policy Award from the Society for Research in Child Development in 1997, and the National Academy of Sciences' Public Welfare Medal in 1998.

Ronald F. Lehman II is Director of the Center for Global Security Research at the Department of Energy's Lawrence Livermore National Laboratory. He works for the University of California and is also Chairman of the Governing Board of the International Science and Technology Center, an intergovernmental organization headquartered in Moscow. He serves as a member of the Department of Defense Threat Reduction Advisory Committee. In 1995, he was appointed to the five-member President's Advisory Board on Arms Proliferation Policy. Previously, he was Director of the U.S. Arms Control and Disarmament Agency from 1989 to 1993. Earlier he served in the Defense Department as Assistant Secretary for International Security Policy, in the State Department as U.S. Chief Negotiator on Strategic Offensive Arms, and in the White House as Deputy Assistant to the President for National Security Affairs. He has also served on the National Security Council staff as a Senior Director, in the Pentagon as Deputy Assistant Secretary, on the professional staff of the U.S. Senate Armed Services Committee, and in Vietnam with the United States Army. He received his B.A. from Claremont McKenna College in 1968 and his Ph.D. from the Claremont Graduate University in 1975. He was a postdoctoral fellow at the Hoover Institution at Stanford University and an Adjunct Professor at Georgetown University.

Thomas E. Lovejoy is Counselor to the Secretary of the Smithsonian Institution for Biodiversity and Environmental Affairs and is currently on a reimbursed detail as Chief Biodiversity Advisor for the World Bank as well as Lead Specialist for Environment for the Latin American and Caribbean region. He holds a B.S. and a Ph.D. (both in biology) from Yale. From 1973 to 1987 he directed the program of the World Wildlife Fund-U.S. and moved to the Smithsonian in 1987 as Assistant Secretary for External Affairs. He served on the White House Science Council in 1988 and the President's Council of Advisors in Science and Technology from 1989 to 1992. In 1993 he served as Science Advisor to the Secretary of the Interior. He co-leads a 20-year-old research project on forest fragmentation in Amazonian Brazil and is active in biodiversity science and conservation.

David D. Newsom received a B.A. from the University of California-Berkeley in 1938 and an M.S. from Columbia University School of Journalism in 1940. After entering the Foreign Service in 1947, he served in Karachi, Oslo, Baghdad, and London. He was appointed Ambassador to Libya in 1965, to Indonesia in 1973, and to the Philippines in 1977. In Washington he served as Officer-in-Charge of Arabian Peninsula Affairs (1955-1960), Director of the Office of Northern African Affairs (1962-1965), Assistant Secretary of State for African Affairs (1969-1973), Undersecretary of State for Political Affairs (1978-1981), and Interim Secretary of State (1981). After his retirement from the Department of State in 1981, he served as Director of the Institute for the Study of Diplomacy and Associate Dean of the School of Foreign Service at Georgetown University. In 1991, he was appointed Cumming Professor of International Studies and Diplomacy at the University of Virginia, a post from which he retired in 1998.

Roland W. Schmitt is President Emeritus, Rensselaer Polytechnic Institute, and Senior Vice President (retired) for Science and Technology, General Electric. He is a past member and Chairman of the National Science Board, the governing body of the National Science Foundation. He is also a member of the National Academy of Engineering, a foreign member of the Royal Swedish Academy of Engineering Sciences, and a foreign associate of the Engineering Academy of Japan. He received his B.A., B.S. (1947), and M.A. (1948) from the University of Texas and his Ph.D. (1951) in physics from Rice University. He is a fellow of the American Physical Society, the American Association for the Advancement of Science, the American Academy of Arts and Sciences, and the Institute of Electrical and Electronics Engineers. He is Chairman-Emeritus of the Board of Governors of the American Institute of Physics and a past Chair of the Council of Scientific Society Presidents. He holds 12 honorary doctorates and Rice University's Distinguished Alumni Award.

Eugene B. Skolnikoff, Professor of Political Science at the Massachusetts Institute of Technology (MIT), has focused his research and teaching interests in the field of international affairs, with a strong emphasis on the political changes brought about by rapid scientific and technological change. He received B.S. and M.S. degrees in electrical engineering at MIT (1950), subsequently a B.A. and M.A. in politics and economics at Oxford studying on a Rhodes Scholarship (1952), and then a Ph.D. in political science from MIT in 1965. He worked on the White House staff in the Office of the Science Adviser in the Eisenhower, Kennedy (1958-1963), and Carter (1977-1981) administrations, dealing there and in his activities at MIT with foreign policy issues. From 1970 to 1974 he was Head of the MIT Political Science Department and from 1972 to 1987 Director of the Center for International Studies. He has also taught at Yale and the Fletcher School at Tufts. He has been a consultant to U.S. Government agencies, including the Departments of State, Energy, and Defense; the National Science Foundation; and the U.S. Congress Office of Technology Assessment, as well as to international organizations, private foundations, and industry. He is presently Chair of the Board of the UN University Institute for New Technology (INTECH) in Maastricht, Holland, and was a member of the Board of Trustees of the German Marshall Fund of the United States, an American foundation, from 1979 to 1987, serving as Chair from 1980 to 1986. He is a fellow of the American Academy of Arts and Sciences and of the American Association for the Advancement of Science. He has published numerous articles and several books, including *The Elusive Transformation: Science, Technology, and the Evolution of International Politics* (Princeton University Press, 1993).

Philip M. Smith, partner, McGeary and Smith, is a science and technology policy advisor and consultant. He chairs the External Advisory Council of the National Computational Science Alliance, is chair or member of other national and international science advisory committees, and serves on corporate boards of small technology startup companies. He was Executive Officer of the National Research Council from 1981 to 1994. He was an Associate Director of the Office of Science and Technology Policy, Executive Office of the President, 1975-1981. Earlier he was the General Science Branch Chief, Office of Management and Budget, and was Director of Geophysical, Oceanographic, and Polar Programs at the National Science Foundation. He is writing a book about science and government with Michael McGeary.

Robert M. White is a principal of the Washington Advisory Group and a Senior Fellow at the University Corporation for Atmospheric Research (UCAR) and the H. John Heinz Center for Science, Economics, and Environment. He was President of the National Academy of Engineering from 1983 to 1995. Prior to that, he was President of UCAR. He was appointed Chief of the U.S. Weather Bureau and was the first Administrator of the National Oceanic and Atmospheric Administration. He was the Karl T. Compton Lecturer at the Massachusetts Institute of Technology in 1995-1996. He has been awarded the Vannevar Bush Award, the Tyler Prize for environmental achievement, the Charles E. Lindbergh Award for technology and environment, the Rockefeller Public Service Award for Protection of Natural Resources, and the International Meteorological Organization Prize.

EX-OFFICIO MEMBERS

David Challoner, Foreign Secretary, Institute of Medicine

Harold Forsen, Foreign Secretary, National Academy of Engineering

F. Sherwood Rowland, Foreign Secretary, National Academy of Sciences

APPENDIX
D

Interim Recommendations of the Committee (September 1998)

NATIONAL RESEARCH COUNCIL

2101 CONSTITUTION AVENUE   WASHINGTON, D. C. 20418

OFFICE OF THE CHAIRMAN

September 11, 1998

The Honorable Madeleine K. Albright
Secretary of State
US Department of State
2201 C Street, NW
Washington, DC 20520

Dear Madam Secretary:

I appreciate the opportunity to respond to your request for a study of the contributions that science, technology, and health (STH) can make to foreign policy, and how the Department might better carry out its responsibilities to that end. With this letter, I enclose the preliminary report that the Department has requested on this important issue.

The opportunities that the areas of science, technology, and health offer in foreign policy are dramatic. As the world leader in most STH areas, the US can build on hundreds of thousands of professional relationships that connect us to the scientific communities in other nations. By forming partnerships with foreign scientists, we enhance their status and support their values, which can do a great deal to promote democracy. In addition, spreading access to new scientific and technical advances is of course essential for providing a decent life and an acceptable environment for the world's expanding population, thereby reducing the potential for destabilizing violent conflicts.

The tasks of understanding and responding to the STH dimensions of foreign policy are daunting. Many officers in political, economic, administrative, and consular positions in Washington and abroad—as well as those with explicit STH responsibilities—must be able to recognize the STH dimensions of foreign affairs. This preliminary report is designed to provide advice on how the Department might best strengthen both its internal STH personnel resources and its utilization of external expertise in pursuing important US security, economic, and scientific goals.

THE NATIONAL RESEARCH COUNCIL IS THE PRINCIPAL OPERATING AGENCY OF THE NATIONAL ACADEMY OF SCIENCES AND THE NATIONAL ACADEMY OF ENGINEERING
TO SERVE GOVERNMENT AND OTHER ORGANIZATIONS.

In outline, the suggestions in the report are as follows:

Providing Leadership within the Department on STH-related Issues

- The Secretary of State should provide continuing leadership for adequate consideration within the Department of the STH aspects of issues and should designate one of the undersecretaries to take the lead in ensuring that STH concerns are considered, when appropriate, during meetings and consultations involving the Secretary's Senior Advisors. This responsibility will require a staff of 2-3 positions that should be located in the office of the designated undersecretary.
- The Department needs several additional clusters of strong STH competence, and it should provide personnel resources for sustained, operational attention to STH content in foreign policy issues.
- The Department should incorporate the STH elements of foreign policy issues and their implications more fully into the Department's strategic planning process.
- The Secretary should articulate and disseminate throughout the Department a policy that calls for greater attention to STH elements of issues in the conduct of foreign affairs and provides guidance as to sources of STH expertise available to both Embassies and Department offices.

Strengthening the Available Base of STH Expertise

- The Department should provide expanded training opportunities for Department officials from the entry level to senior levels for developing and strengthening STH-related competencies.
- Attractive career incentives are needed for FSOs to actively seek assignments involving STH-related issues at both senior and junior levels.
- The Department should enhance the technical stature and capabilities of US Embassies in countries where STH developments are of special importance through assignment of technically trained personnel to Science Counselor and other full-time science positions.
- The Department should systematize the exchange of personnel with STH skills with other US agencies that have strong capabilities in STH.
- The Department should expand its pool of external experts and actively engage them in advising the Department's leadership on emerging STH issues.

little or no cost, while some involve the assignment or establishment of up to about twelve positions to STH purposes. Creating the most ambitious advisory mechanism that the Committee has so far considered might involve the expenditure of $500,000 annually. These seem modest investments given the stakes involved.

In addition to providing a broad vision for the role of STH in foreign policy, the further work of this committee will explore in more detail three sets of issues: general personnel policies and practices; the clusters of STH expertise in the foreign affairs agencies; and the STH-related international activities of other departments and agencies.

In order to best meet your needs, I would like to meet with you to receive your guidance concerning the most important aspects of these or other issues that we should address in the next phase of this study. You may also wish to identify a specific current foreign policy issue with major STH components where advice is needed. We would be pleased to assemble a small group of experts to explore -- with yourself, the committee, and appropriate State officers -- both the issue and the role of STH advice in dealing with it.

I look forward to continuing the interactions with you and your colleagues as the committee prepares more detailed recommendations and the supporting documentation for your consideration.

Sincerely,

Bruce Alberts
Chairman
National Research Council
and
President
National Academy of Sciences

APPENDIX

E

Senate Act 886:
Foreign Relations Authorization Act,
Fiscal Years 2000 and 2001

**Section 303. SCIENCE AND TECHNOLOGY ADVISER TO THE
SECRETARY OF STATE**

(a) ESTABLISHMENT OF POSITION. – Section 1 of the State Department Basic Authorities Act of 1956 (22 U.S.C. 2651a) is
amended by adding at the end the following new subsection:

(g) SCIENCE AND TECHNOLOGY ADVISER. –

(1) IN GENERAL. – There shall be within the Department of
State a Science and Technology Adviser (in this paragraph
referred to as the 'Adviser'). The Adviser shall report to the
Secretary of State through the Under Secretary for Global
Affairs.

(2) DUTIES. – The Adviser shall –

(A) advise the Secretary of State, through the Under Secretary of State for Global Affairs, on international science
and technology matters affecting the foreign policy of the
United States; and

(B) perform such duties, exercise such powers, and have such
rank and status as the Secretary of State shall prescribe.

(b) REPORT. – Not later than six months after receipt by the Secretary
of State of the report by the National Research Council of the National
Academy of Sciences with respect to the contributions that science,
technology, and health matters can make to the foreign policy of the

United States, the Secretary of State, acting through the Under Secretary of State for Global Affairs, shall submit a report to Congress setting forth the Secretary of State's plans for implementation, as appropriate, of the recommendations of the report.

Section 612. ASSISTANT SECRETARY OF STATE FOR VERIFICATION AND COMPLIANCE

(a) DESIGNATION OF POSITION – The Secretary of State shall designate one of the Assistant Secretaries of State authorized by section 1(c)(1) of the State Department Basic Authorities Act of 1956 (22 U.S.C. 2651a(c)(1)) as the Assistant Secretary of State for Verification and Compliance. The Assistant Secretary shall report to the Under Secretary of State for Arms Control and International Security.

(b) DIRECTIVE GOVERNING THE ASSISTANT SECRETARY OF STATE –
   (1) IN GENERAL – Not later than 30 days after the date of enactment of this Act, the Secretary of State shall issue a directive governing the position of Assistant Secretary.

(c) DUTIES –

   (1) IN GENERAL – The Assistant Secretary shall have as his principal responsibility the overall supervision (including oversight of policy and resources) within the Department of State of all matters relating to verification and compliance with international arms control, nonproliferation, and disarmament agreements or commitments.
   (2) PARTICIPATION OF THE ASSISTANT SECRETARY –
      (A) PRIMARY ROLE – Except as provided in subparagraphs (B) and (C), the Assistant Secretary, or his designee, shall participate in all interagency groups or organizations within the executive branch of Government that assess, analyze, or review United States planned or ongoing policies, programs, or actions that have a direct bearing on verification or compliance matters, including interagency intelligence committees concerned with the development or exploitation of measurement or signals intelligence or other national technical means of verification.
      (B) REQUIREMENT FOR DESIGNATION – Subparagraph (A) shall not apply to groups or organizations on which

the Secretary of State of the Undersecretary of State for Arms Control and International Security sits, unless such official designates the Assistant Secretary to attend in his stead.

(C) NATIONAL SECURITY LIMITATION –

(i) The President may waive the provisions of subparagraph (A) if inclusion of the Assistant Secretary would not be in the national security interests of the United States.

(ii) With respect to an interagency group or organization, or meeting thereof, working with exceptionally sensitive information contained in compartments under the control of the Director of Central Intelligence, the Secretary of Defense, or the Secretary of Energy, such Director or Secretary, as the case may be, may waive the provision of subparagraph (A) if inclusion of the Assistant Secretary would not be in the national security interests of the United States.

(iii) Any waiver of participation under clause (i) or (ii) shall be transmitted in writing to the appropriate committees of Congress.

(3) RELATIONSHIP TO THE INTELLIGENCE COMMUNITY – The Assistant Secretary shall be the principal liaison between the policy community and the intelligence community on verification and compliance matters.

APPENDIX
F

Affiliations of U.S. Government Officials and Other Specialists Consulted by Committee and Staff

U.S. Department of State

Office of the Secretary of State
    Policy Planning Staff
    Office of Resources, Plans, and Policy
    Bureau of Intelligence and Research
        Office of the Deputy Assistant Secretary for Analysis
        Office of the Geographer and Global Issues
    Office of the Legal Adviser

Office of the Deputy Secretary of State

Office of the Undersecretary of State for Political Affairs
    Bureau of Inter-American Affairs (now Bureau of Western Hemisphere Affairs)
    Bureau of International Organization Affairs
    Bureau of East Asian and Pacific Affairs
    Bureau of African Affairs

Office of the Undersecretary of State for Management
    Foreign Service Institute
    Bureau of Information Resource Management
    Bureau of Personnel

Office of the Director General of the Foreign Service/
    Director of Personnel
Office of Career Development and Assignments
Office of Civil Service Personnel Management
Office of Overseas Employment
Office of Performance Evaluation
Office of Recruitment, Examination, and Employment
Policy Coordination Staff

Office of the Undersecretary for Arms Control and International Security
    Bureau of Nonproliferation
        Office of Regional Nonproliferation
        Office of Nuclear Energy Affairs
        Office of Proliferation Threat Reduction
        Office of Export Controls and Conventional Arms
            Nonproliferation Policy
    Bureau of Political-Military Affairs
    Nuclear Safeguards and Technology Division, Nonproliferation and
        Regional Arms Control Bureau, Arms Control and Disarmament
        Agency[1]

Office of the Undersecretary for Economic, Business, and Agricultural
Affairs
    Bureau of Economic and Business Affairs
        Office of International Energy and Commodity Policy
    Office of the Deputy Assistant Secretary for International
            Communications and Information Policy
    Office of Strategic Planning/Satellites
    Office of International Trade (Multilateral Trade Agreements)

Office of the Undersecretary for Global Affairs
    Bureau of Oceans and International Environmental and
            Scientific Affairs
        Office of the Executive Director
        Office of Policy Coordination and Initiatives
        Office of Science and Technology Cooperation
        Emerging and Infectious Disease and AIDS Staff
        Office of Oceans Affairs

---

[1]This office was consulted prior to the incorporation of ACDA into the Department in
April 1999.

        Office of Marine Conservation
        Space and Advanced Technology Staff
        Office of Global Change
        Office of Ecology and Terrestrial Conservation
        Office of Environmental Policy
    Bureau of Population, Refugees, and Migration

Office of the Counselor of the Department of State

Other Government Offices and Agencies

Office of Science and Technology Policy

Office of Management and Budget

U.S. Agency for International Development
    Bureau for Global Programs, Field Support, and Research
        Office of Health and Nutrition
        Center for Environment
        Center for Economic Growth and Agricultural Development
    Bureau for Policy and Program Coordination
        Office of the Senior Policy Group
    Bureau for Latin America and the Caribbean
        Office of Strategy and Portfolio Management
    Bureau for Africa
    Bureau for Europe and the New Independent States
    Bureau for Humanitarian Response
    Bureau for Asia and the Near East
    Office of Human Resources

U.S. Information Agency
    Office of the Director
        Office of Strategic Communication
    Bureau of Educational and Cultural Affairs
        Office of Exchange Coordination
        Office of Policy and Evaluation
        Working Group on U.S. Government International Exchanges and
            Training
    Bureau of Management
        Office of Human Resources
    Bureau of Information
        Office of Thematic Programs (Global Issues and Communications)

U.S. Department of Energy
   Office of Nonproliferation and National Security

National Science Foundation
   Division of International Programs

U.S. House of Representatives, Committee on Science

National Aeronautics and Space Administration
   Office of External Relations

National Institutes of Health
   Fogarty International Center, Division of International Relations
   National Institute of Child Health and Human Development

U.S. Department of Health and Human Services
   Office of International Health
   Office of International Reproductive Health
   Centers for Disease Control and Prevention
   Office of Global Health, Policy Coordination Unit

U.S. Food and Drug Administration
   Office of International Affairs

Defense Intelligence Agency

National Oceanic and Atmospheric Administration
   Office of International Affairs
   Office of Oceanic and Atmospheric Research
   National Marine Fisheries Service
   National Environmental Satellite, Data, and Information Service
   Office of International and Interagency Affairs

U.S. Environmental Protection Agency
   Office of the Assistant Administrator for International Activities

U.S. Department of Commerce
   U.S.-Israel Science and Technology Commission
   Office of Air and Space Commercialization
   Technology Administration
   National Technical Information Service

Other Organizations and Specialists

American Federation of Government Employees

American Foreign Service Association

Robert Gallucci, Dean, Georgetown University School of Foreign Service

John Gibbons, former Director, Office of Science and Technology Policy

William Golden, Co-chair, Carnegie Commission on Science and Government

Larry Kanarek, McKinsey & Company

J. Thomas Ratchford, Director, Center for Science, Technology, and Trade Policy, George Mason University

Adm. James D. Watkins (USN, ret.), President, Consortium for Oceanographic Research and Education

Group of State EST Counselors and Officers

Panel of young FSOs in EST positions

Panel of former EST Counselors

APPENDIX
G

International Affairs Strategic Goals[1]

• Regional Stability: Strengthen the security of the United States and prevent instabilities from threatening the vital and important interests of the United States and its allies.

• **Weapons of Mass Destruction: Reduce the threat to the United States and its allies from weapons of mass destruction.**

• Open Markets: Open world markets to increase trade and free the flow of goods, services, and capital.

• U.S. Exports: Expand U.S. exports to $1.2 trillion early in the twenty-first century.

• Global Growth and Stability: Increase global economic growth and stability.

• Economic Development: Promote broad-based growth in developing and transitional economies to raise standards of living and lessen disparities of wealth within and among countries.

---

[1]Goals with STH content are highlighted in bold.

• American Citizens: Protect the safety and security of American citizens who travel and live abroad.

• Travel and Migration: Manage fairly and effectively the entry of immigrants and foreign visitors into the United States.

• **International Crime: Minimize the impact of international crime on the United States and its citizens.**

• **Illegal Drugs: Reduce the entry of illegal drugs into the United States.**

• **Counterterrorism: Reduce the number and impact of international terrorist attacks, especially on the United States and its citizens.**

• Democracy and Human Rights: Open political systems and societies to democratic practices, the rule of law, good governance, and respect for human rights.

• **Humanitarian Assistance: Prevent or minimize the human costs of conflict and natural disasters.**

• **Environment: Secure a sustainable global environment and protect the United States and its citizens from the effects of international environmental degradation.**

• **Population: Achieve a sustainable world population.**

• **Health: Protect human health and reduce the spread of infectious diseases.**

SOURCE: "United States Strategic Plan for International Affairs, First Revision," released by the Office of Resources, Plans, and Policy, U.S. Department of State, Washington, D.C., February 1999. See <http://www.state.gov/www/global/general_foreign_policy/99_stratplan_toc.html>.

Standard Field Position Description— Scientific and Technological Affairs Officer

Summary

Serves as Counselor for Scientific and Technological Affairs or S&T Attaché in a mission when international oceans and environmental affairs, science, and technology have a significant impact on foreign policy issues.

General Duties

Advises the Chief of Mission and the country team about significant scientific, technological, environmental and oceans policies, programs and developments which are relevant to U.S. policies and objectives in the host country. Specific topics include: space research, development, and applications; toxic chemicals; nuclear and non-nuclear energy research and development; non-proliferation; marine sciences; technology transfer; nuclear export controls; population matters; joint S&T projects; and scientific exchanges.

Provides an appropriate analysis and evaluation of these developments and participates actively in the formulation of policy recommendations which take full account of the scientific and technological aspects of foreign policy issues in the economic, political, security, and public affairs areas.

Implements agreed U.S. policies in host country. Serves as the key Embassy liaison officer for all contacts with the most senior officials of host country science ministries, institutions, and organizations. Makes appropriate representations in support of U.S. policy; as instructed, negotiates any agreements required; and reports on the status of Embassy programs designed to achieve U.S. policy objectives. Because of the high level and wide variety of the contacts, has heavy representational responsibility.

Identifies scientific and technological areas of mutual interest to both countries which are suitable for bilateral collaboration of which may be incorporated in multilateral programs for cooperation to achieve political, economic, or security objectives of regional or worldwide scope.

Analyzes and evaluates the technologies involved, recommends appropriate initiatives, and conducts necessary negotiations. Serves as the principal point of contact in the Embassy for the U.S. technical agencies involved in the cooperative programs.

Prepares reports on significant S&T policies and developments in host country. These reports include studies in direct support of major policy formulation, ongoing negotiations, and other activities related to policy implementation. May also prepare in-depth analytical and evaluative reports on major trends in science, technology and environmental affairs as they affect the economic and political aspects of U.S. foreign policy in general and the specific U.S. objectives in the host country.

In coordination with other elements of the Embassy, supports U.S. commercial interests especially among the advanced technology industries by assisting U.S. businessmen in understanding local customs, laws, procurement practices, rules and regulations relating to technology transfer, advising them about potential markets and technological capabilities of the host country, and by helping them to make contacts at appropriate levels in host government ministries and the private sector.

Represents the Embassy in contacts with the host country S&T community in order to explain U.S. policies, to explore new areas for S&T cooperation and exchanges, and to develop a meaningful dialogue between the host country and the U.S.

Represents the Embassy, the Department of State, and other agencies at scientific and technological meetings and similar activities. Arranges for the Ambassador's participation where appropriate and prepares statements for delivery before such groups.

Travels extensively within the geographic region to establish and maintain contacts with other diplomatic posts, host government officials, regional authorities, academic scientists, industries, and other representatives of the private sector.

Where technical representatives of other agencies are assigned to Embassies abroad, they may form an integral part of the Science and Technology Section of the Embassy. Coordinates the activities of such representatives in order to provide them with foreign policy guidance and to ensure their full participation in the overall goals and objectives established for the U.S. mission. The S&T Affairs Specialist and the other agency representatives work as a team to make the maximum contribution to U.S. foreign policy goals and objectives. At the discretion of the Ambassador, the S&T Section of the Embassy may also include officers with other related responsibilities; for example, energy policy, mineral resources, and fisheries attachés.

Serves as coordinator for significant S&T visits and missions. Assists in organizing and facilitating such visits to assure an optimum return from the contacts. Participates in the visits as appropriate to provide a foreign policy perspective for the mission and to permit any necessary follow-up.

Acts as the focal point within the Embassy for all binational S&T agreements and arrangements, whether intergovernmental or inter-agency. Promotes, facilitates, and monitors such agreements to further U.S. policy objectives and essential relationships. Serves as the liaison between the numerous U.S. technical agencies and their foreign counterparts, and reviews, approves, and provides administrative support for research projects within the host country supported by American agencies. Represents the Embassy in developing guidelines and operating procedures for cooperative programs and briefs visiting agency representatives on the political, economic, or public relations aspects for their specific programs.

A working knowledge of the language of the host country is often a necessity for science officers at all levels.

SOURCE: OES, Department of State, 1999.

APPENDIX

I

Goals, Strategies, and Objectives in the Program Plan of the Bureau of Oceans and International Environmental and Scientific Affairs

Melinda L. Kimble, Acting Assistant Secretary[1]

GOAL 1: Conserve and sustainably manage terrestrial, marine, and atmospheric resources, including the earth's climate system

Strategy

The U.S. Government will engage in a range of activities that include bilateral, regional, and multilateral negotiations; implementation of international agreements; bilateral and regional dialogues with key countries; and bilateral and regional activities that improve the capabilities of developing countries and promote regional cooperation on transboundary environmental issues. Many of the regional and bilateral activities will be focused on building or sustaining coalitions that support U.S. positions and advance our interests in international negotiations. Details of specific activities, treaty negotiations, and cooperative initiatives are given below; some examples of key activities include:

• Participation in the Tropical Forests Conservation Act, Commission on Sustainable Development, and International Coral Reef Initiative to promote innovative mechanisms for sustainable management of key ecosystems.
• Participation in the 6th Conference of the Parties [COP-6] to achieve

---

[1]Presented in July 1999. This material was extracted from the OES internal program plan, which also discusses past accomplishments and administrative issues.

international agreement on rules and guidelines for components of the Kyoto Protocol.

• Use of bilateral projects or regional workshops to promote mutually supportive relations between trade and sustainable management of ecosystems.

• Implementation of existing agreements to promote sustainable fisheries and protect marine ecosystems including the implementation of the Global Program of Action.

Objectives

• Promote innovative mechanisms for sustainable management of key marine and terrestrial ecosystems, including the polar caps and freshwater resources.

• Achieve international agreement on rules and guidelines on the components of the Kyoto Protocol, and continue implementation of the Montreal Protocol.

• Protect the marine environment and endangered marine species, with a special emphasis on marine pollution and fisheries management.

• Reduce transboundary air and water pollution through cooperative efforts with Canada, Mexico, and ECE [Eastern and Central European] countries.

• Safeguard and promote U.S. environmental interests in the context of trade and economic liberalization efforts.

• Promote international collaboration in the use of space technologies for environmental monitoring and humanitarian response.

GOAL 2: Reduce health and environmental risks from toxic chemicals, hazardous wastes, and the emergence and spread of infectious diseases

Strategy

To promote the safe management of toxic chemicals and hazardous wastes and to address the spread of infectious disease, the U.S. Government will engage in a range of activities that include bilateral, regional, and multilateral negotiations; implementation of international agreements; bilateral and regional dialogues; and capacity-building activities to promote regional cooperation on transboundary environmental issues, including:

• Fund, and participate in, meetings related to the implementation of the Prior Informed Consent (PIC) Convention.

- Sponsor capacity-building activities related to the reduction or elimination of persistent organic pollutants.
- Participate in global and regional activities to reduce and manage risks to the environment and human health associated with international shipments and disposal of hazardous wastes.
- Implement the Secretary of State's Action Plan for the Diplomatic Initiative on HIV/AIDS.

Objectives

- Reduce or eliminate releases of persistent organic pollutants into the environment and promote the sound management of chemicals globally.
- Reduce and manage risks to human health and environment associated with the international shipment and disposal of hazardous waste.
- Strengthen political commitment for enhanced global preparedness against infectious diseases.

GOAL 3: Promote open access to areas beyond national jurisdiction, including the oceans and space, in accordance with international law

Strategy

The U.S. Government will engage in a range of activities that include bilateral, regional, and multilateral negotiations; key country accession and international compliance with agreements and norms; and capacity building of enforcement and monitoring organizations. Details of specific activities, treaty negotiations, and cooperative initiatives are given below; some examples of key activities are:

- Working with the Northwest Atlantic Fisheries Organization and International Commission on the Conservation of Atlantic Tuna (ICCAT) to maintain and promote fishing opportunities for U.S. fisheries.
- Supporting the UN Convention on the Law of the Sea.
- Participating in multilateral discussions (e.g., World Radio Communication Conference) to promote the acceptance of the U.S. Global Positioning System as the worldwide standard for satellite-based navigation services.
- Through bilateral S&T agreements, promote U.S. Government access to foreign S&T institutions and establishments in areas that support U.S. environment, health, economic, and security interests.

Objectives

- Maintain and promote fishing opportunities for U.S. fisheries.
- Promote acceptance of the U.S. Global Positioning System (GPS) as a worldwide standard for satellite-based navigation services.
- Devise bilateral and multilateral agreements to ensure U.S. access to space.
- Implement international law concerning ocean jurisdiction as reflected in the provisions of the Law of the Sea Convention.

GOAL 4:   Strengthen bilateral and regional relationships and multilateral institutions to advance, broadly, the goals of the Bureau

Strategy

The U.S. Government will engage in a range of activities that build bilateral and regional relationships. These may include technology transfer, science and technology cooperation, or the funding of and participation in workshops, meetings and conferences. Many of these activities will focus on integrating U.S. Government environment and health goals with broader political, economic, humanitarian and security-related interests. EST and regional environmental officers are a necessary component to achieving this mission. Some examples of targeted activities:

- Use existing bilateral relationships or regional fora—such as APEC [Asia Pacific Economic Cooperation Forum], ASEAN [Association of Southeast Asian Nations], or the EU [European Union]—to communicate U.S. Government environment, health and science goals and objectives to key countries, including China, Japan, Kazakhstan, Mexico, Brazil, Russia and Ukraine.
- Develop new and expand nascent dialogues with key countries and regional mechanisms to advance U.S. Government environment, health and science interests. Countries and regional organizations include Egypt, India, South Africa, Columbia, the South Asia Association for Regional Cooperation (SAARC), and the Southern African Development Community (SADC).
- Broadly promote U.S. interests by participating in and supporting the Global Environment Facility, UNEP [United Nations Environment Programme], Intergovernmental Panel on Climate Change [IPCC], UN Framework Convention on Climate Change, UN Committee on Sustainable Development, and OECD Environmental Policy Committee.

Objectives

• Create new and utilize existing regularly planned dialogues with key countries to advance EST&H interests, and increase capacity of those managing the EST portfolio at post to manage environmental diplomacy relationships.

• Enhance regional engagements through regional environmental hubs and EST officers at post to advance U.S. Government environment, oceans, science, technology and health goals, and to help regions respond to environmental challenges.

• Safeguard and promote U.S. environmental and health interests worldwide through cooperative efforts in multilateral (e.g., OECD, UNEP, IPCC, CSD), financial (e.g., Global Environment Facility) and scientific institutions.

GOAL 5: Ensure that science informs, and is integrated into, the conduct of U.S. foreign policy, and promote interests of the U.S. scientific community

Strategy

The Department of State will employ several methods to better integrate science and technology into foreign policy decision-making. In addition to consultations with expert technical agencies, academic institutions, international scientific bodies, and nongovernmental organizations, the Department of State will employ a special "science" advisor to facilitate the exchange of information between scientists and the foreign policy community. The Department will also utilize existing, and if necessary advocate new, multinational scientific organizations to advise policymakers on important foreign policy issues. Examples of key activities include:

• Establish a science advisor within the Department of State to facilitate the integration of science into foreign policy decision making.

• Support international scientific institutions such as the Intergovernmental Panel on Climate Change (IPCC), Global Climate Observing System (GCOS), International Commission for the Exploration of the Sea (ICES), the North Pacific Marine Research Organization (PICES), and the Intergovernmental Oceanographic Commission (IOC).

Objectives

- Improve integration of the science of climate change into U.S. foreign policy.
- Improve integration of marine science into U.S. foreign policy.
- Establish a science advisor within the Department of State to facilitate the integration of science into foreign policy decision-making.
- Expand bilateral S&T cooperation with key countries to build support for U.S. Government positions on environment, oceans, science, technology, and health issues.
- Improve flora and fauna information systems to support science-based ecosystem management and policy-making.

GOAL 6: Increase public diplomacy and outreach

Strategy

Conduct comprehensive public diplomacy and public affairs strategies to explain U.S. positions on key OES issues. Activities will include press relations; outreach to nongovernmental organizations, business and industry representatives, and other targeted audiences; and the distribution of public information on U.S. Government policies. OES must have the personnel, infrastructure, and technology necessary to communicate U.S. policy interests around the world.

Objectives

- Establish an adequate infrastructure to support the Bureau's newly integrated public diplomacy function and OES international and domestic outreach operations.
- Increase bureau-wide and Department-wide awareness of and engagement in public diplomacy and outreach activities that support EST&H policy objectives.
- Conduct public diplomacy and provide on-site international media relations support to U.S. delegations during COP-6 of the UN Framework Convention on Climate Change and during negotiations related to persistent organic pollutants.